TEACHING STRINGED INSTRUMENTS IN CLASSES

ELIZABETH A.H. GREEN

Printed in the United States of America for the American String Teachers Association

1999 Printing
Copyright © 1966 by Elixabeth A. H. Green

ISBN 0-89917-507-4

ACKNOWLEDGMENTS

Though copyrighted in 1966 by Elizabeth A.H. Green and published by the American String Teachers Association in 1987, the material in this book has stood the test of time and is as fresh and applicable today as the day it was written. Acceptance by string and orchestra teachers is as strong now as it was thirty years ago. Thus, the need for this reprinting.

A few minor changes have been made: Daniel Long, former Elizabeth Green student and successful music educator, has written a beautiful tribute to Ms. Green; pictures have all been reshot; text has been produced in digital format for clarity and sharpness; the cover has been redesigned and a spiral binding added to make for easier usage.

Robert H. Klotman was the ASTA Publications Chair at the time of the initial printing in 1987. He graciously agreed to supervise the production of the new pictures. A former president of both ASTA and MENC, Bob has continued in a variety of ways to perform valuable service to the music profession in his retirement.

Models chosen for the pictures are: Jordana Greenberg, Gina Welch, Julie Rubinger and Robin Scott. We are appreciative of the time and effort they volunteered to help make this new printing up-to-date. It just so happens that Robin Scott's mother, Sylvia Scott, studied with Elizabeth Green at the University of Michigan. What a wonderful historical happenstance to have a personal connection between this new printing of Elizabeth Green's book and the author herself.

Anne Sheldon served ably as proof reader. Her time and careful approach to the text are much appreciated.

This book is but one of many monuments that Elizabeth Green left us. It will aid the string teachers of the future, I am confident, just as it has informed and inspired those from the past.

Robert L. Cowden
ASTA with NSOA Publications Chair

ELIZABETH A. H. GREEN:
A TRIBUTE
1906-1995

Elizabeth A. H. Green, internationally renowned teacher, and author of numerous books and publications on strings, conducting, and music education, died September 25, 1995, at her home in Ann Arbor, Michigan. She was 89.

Elizabeth Adine Herkimer Green was born in Mobile, Alabama, in 1906. Her family moved to Chicago when she was two years old. She began studying the violin with her father when she was three. In 1919 the Greens moved to Wheaton, Illinois, where her father taught violin at Wheaton College.

In 1928 Miss Green was graduated from Wheaton College. Her first conducting experience occurred during her senior year when she conducted the Wheaton Academy Orchestra. She spent the next fourteen years in Waterloo, Iowa, teaching at East High School (the school's auditorium was dedicated and named the Elizabeth A.H. Green Auditorium in 1997). She was a founding member of the Waterloo Symphony, and she fulfilled whatever role was most needed: principal viola, principal string bass, later concertmaster. In 1939 she received a Master of Music degree from Northwestern University. She studied with Jacques Gordon, former concertmaster of the Chicago Symphony Orchestra, and Clarence Evans, principal viola of the CSO. It was through these teachers that Green began studying conducting with the great Russian master, Nicolai Malko, in 1941. Thus began a career that included concertmaster, judge, author, and, most significantly, the roles of mentor and teacher.

Miss Green came to Ann Arbor in 1942 as an assistant professor of music education at The University of Michigan and Director of Orchestras at Ann Arbor High School and Slauson Junior High School. She held these positions for the next ten years, at which time she became Professor of Music Education at The University of Michigan. During her years in Ann Arbor she played in the Saginaw Symphony, Detroit Womens Symphony, and was concertmaster of the Ann Arbor Symphony for over twenty years.

In 1961 Professor Green authored *The Modern Conductor*. Based on Nicolai Malko's pedagogy it has become a standard text for the study of conducting. The manuscript for the sixth edition (published in 1997) was completed just before she died. Green also completed Malko's *The Conductor and His Score*, in 1975. She served as a judge for the prestigious Nicolai Malko Competition, held every three years in Copenhagen.

Between the summers of 1947 and 1955, Green studied violin with Ivan Galamian at Meadowmount Music School. In 1961, after her persistent prodding and with her assistance, Galamian set down his violin philosophy in *Principles of Violin Playing and Teaching*. Miss Green maintained a close relationship with Galamian's widow and at the request of Mrs. Galamian in 1993 she published the biography: *Miraculous Teacher: Ivan Galamian and the Meadowmount Experience*.

"She has left a wonderful heritage beyond measure. Elizabeth has left something incredible in this world," said Ivan Galamian's widow, Judith. "I was just a small town, country girl, that became part of a magnificent team--three people who came from different parts of the world to form a trilogy of significant stature. Ivan and Elizabeth were the brains and creative forces in my life. Had it not been for Elizabeth, my husband's book would not have happened. She is and will continue to be a permanent fixture."

Professor Green retired from The University of Michigan in 1975 with an avalanche of awards and honors and the title of Professor Emerita. She subsequently enrolled at Eastern Michigan University, where she studied painting, and in 1978 was awarded a bachelor's degree in art.

Elizabeth's influence is far-reaching, tucked into places all over the world. One particular meeting comes to mind. She arrived with a burst of laughter. "You will never believe this letter," she said. "Here, let me read it to you." And she began to read a long letter from an Indian sailor who was at sea in the Indian Ocean. He had found a copy of *The Modern Conductor* in the ship's library and was so taken by her book that he wanted to become a conductor. Apparently he was going to be at sea for six months and wanted to know if that would be enough time to learn the "art of conducting." Did she have any advice? After a few moments she began to give this request some serious thought. She never turned down a challenge. She made a long list of books and recordings, a few conducting exercises and sent them off with a P.S.: "When you get home, find an orchestra. You cannot be a conductor without an orchestra."

When it came to music and conducting, she was uncompromising. There was no substitute for excellence. Elizabeth was a stickler for detail--down to the smallest gesture. Everything was done correctly. On March 22, 1995, the Michigan House of Representatives passed Resolution No.91 recognizing her contributions. She was hailed "a world famous educator, musician, conductor and author." It was a great honor and she was moved. But, when she read the resolution it was for Elizabeth A. Green. "How could those folks in Lansing (state capital) make such a terrible mistake," she jested. Later someone said, "Miss Green, you have been giving away 'H' for almost seventy years. It was finally put down in print." Her response: "The world is filled with Elizabeth A. Greens but there is only one Elizabeth A. H. Green." Truer words were never spoken. She did get a corrected copy of that resolution.

Elizabeth Green devoted much of her research and reading on studies of the brain and how the mind functions. In almost every lecture or demonstration she gave there was reference to the intellectual capacities of the mind, brain power that needed to be tapped, or the importance of connecting the notes on the page to the heart through the brain and its great strength. She often spoke of what learning to play an instrument does to the development of the brain. "Playing an instrument develops the whole brain--making sure we do not have students who are half-brained!" Numerous articles and studies are making the headlines today revealing the impact music has on the brain. A great discovery? Elizabeth Green knew over thirty years ago what some scientists are just discovering today. "Music is the greatest instrument for mental hygiene in the curriculum. It requires eyes, mind, ears, and muscular response to work together in split-record accuracy. It develops the whole man, because, in addition to the physical-mental-physical reactions, it is colored with the great emotional meaning of life itself." (Elizabeth A.H. Green, "Is Music Worth the Price?" *The Instrumentalist*, April 1962, p.34).

Elizabeth Green was always on the cutting edge. She never stopped learning and was always searching for new ideas. Eager to learn, she was ever on the quest to uncover one more technic that would help solve another problem. A few years ago she fractured her right arm. After several weeks of immobility she began the slow progress of playing again. Through this experience she got the idea that a book needed to be written on "how to practice." In addition to completing the sixth edition of *The Modern Conductor*, she spent the last few months of her life writing yet one more book, *Practicing Successfully*. She did in her last year what most do not do in a lifetime.

Although she was extremely modest, Miss Green was admired widely by some of the world's greatest musicians and even more so in the hearts of her students. She was a master teacher who had the highest hopes and expectations for all of us, and she did not rest until she had taught, inspired, encouraged, motivated, and reassured those of us who were her students and friends.

Each one of us is a collection of those who have entered into our lives. Elizabeth Green has had a tremendous influence on many people. Knowing her has enriched our lives beyond words. She was a very special person, a legendary star that will never go out. We all share a part of a great woman that shall be passed on for generations. Her warmth, friendliness, love, and caring will live forever. She taught the love of music and of life itself.

E. Daniel Long

PREFACE

The class-method approach to instrumental music in the public school has provided the profession with a vast laboratory for research on how children best learn to become proficient on musical instruments. It has also brought into focus many divergent pedagogical ideas, correlating and refining them, until today there is much more agreement on what comprises good technique and what are the important things in building it.

A teacher need no longer be poorly informed about what is feasible on the violin, viola, cello, or string bass. Works dealing with the specifics for each of these instruments have been published, but very little has been written on the teaching of all four instruments simultaneously in one class. The purpose of this book is to set forth and to distinguish between the heterogeneous and homogeneous approaches in such a way that all members of the heterogeneous class can continue to progress during their mutual class period with as little waste of time as possible.

Daily classes during the first two or three weeks of instruction put the children and the program far ahead, both technically and chronologically. For the remainder of the first year, classes meeting twice a week are adequate. Home practice should be delayed until after the youngsters have set good hand positions, can draw straight bows, and play one or more tunes well by rote.

Teaching the several stringed instruments simultaneously is like plaiting a braid. Each strand must be handled skillfully, must progress logically in its own direction, and must be kept moving forward so that the final product is both symmetrical and secure. There must be no thin spots along the way.

Elizabeth A.H. Green
1966

TABLE OF CONTENTS

TEACHING STRINGED
INSTRUMENTS IN CLASSES

CHAPTER ONE
BEGINNING THE INSTRUCTION

S trings are not harder to teach than winds. Whereas the problem of the beginning wind player is that of building range, note by note, the problem of the string novice is the bi-manual functioning of his hands, each doing a specialized type of work, but each having to correlate with the other so that while functioning individually they can also work effectively together. For this reason the methodology for the beginning string class differs vitally from that for the beginning wind class. The wind player will start the reading of music much sooner. The string player will play by rote and by ear for an appreciable period before going to the music. But once he begins his reading he will progress by leaps and bounds so that, at the end of the first year's study, winds and strings will be efficiently comparable in the amount of skill developed in their unique fields of endeavor.

The road to mastery in the strings is somewhat longer than that for the winds. For example, the technique of double-stop and chord playing, the production of harmonics as such, and the many kinds of staccatos (martelé, slurred, spiccato, sautillé, volante, ricochet — each a specialized technique in itself) contribute to the lengthening of the period of study needed to become proficient. But the road can be interesting and fascinating most of the way.

With these brief introductory remarks, let us proceed immediately to the business at hand, namely, the teaching of the stringed instruments in the class situation. Since the more difficult teaching problems occur in the class of mixed strings, the heterogeneous class, this book will deal with the methodology for such a situation, showing wherein the teaching technique may correlate violins, violas, cellos and basses, and in which aspects of the instruction they must be given individualized attention.

Before the first class convenes each youngster should be provided with an instrument of the correct size ($^1/_4$, $^1/_2$, $^3/_4$, or full size).[1] Figure 1-1 shows the recommended method for measuring the child's arm on violin or viola. When the fingers of the left hand can curl around the scroll with the instrument in the pictured position, then in playing position there will be sufficient bend in the elbow to permit the fingers to reach easily their correct pitches on the several strings. The requisite for the young cellist is that his first and fourth fingers, when placed on the D string, should be able to span the interval of the major third (E to G-sharp). For the string bass, the youngster's first to fourth finger should encompass one whole tone, and most essential, the bass should be adjusted in height so that the nut (over which the strings pass as they enter the peg-box) stands at a position opposite the child's forehead. This permits his left hand to reach playing position without strain and also allows the bow arm to position the bow correctly on the string without an ungainly bend in the elbow.

For youngsters who wish to study viola, if small sized instruments are not available, the strings on a violin of the correct size may be changed around so that it temporarily becomes a viola. This is not good tonally, but it enables the child to start his viola work immediately, and time takes care of the rest of the problem.

Figure 1-1. Measuring the arm on the violin.

[1]The standard sized bass is the $^3/_4$. Full sized basses are very rare.

Note: We earnestly advise *no home practice* until after these first ten lessons are completed in the supervised classes.

THE FIRST LESSON

The children come eagerly into the room. Their greatest desire is to get the new instrument into their hands and to begin to make it sound. If the class is large, the teacher may wish to tune only the D and A strings, thereby saving time for the real instruction.

Note: Some teachers prefer to start the instruction with the use of the bow; others like to set the left hand and begin with ear-training and the plucking of the D scale and perhaps a bit of a tune. We shall set forth here the routines for the first two classes with the premise that either one of the two could furnish the material for the very first class, with the other becoming the second lesson. Two or more classes a week are imperative in beginning work.

THE INITIAL INTRODUCTION TO THE INSTRUMENT

The children are asked to pick up their instruments and to turn the strings toward themselves so that they can "take a good look at them." The violins and violas will stand upright on the child's knee, strings facing the player. The youngsters playing cellos and basses will rotate them until their strings are also facing the players.

The teacher now plucks the A string on his own instrument (or plays it on the piano) and asks the children to "find the string that sounds the same" on their instruments. This approach tells the child nothing, but instead requires him to *use his own ears to solve successfully his first problem.* The immediate activating of the ear is imperative in all stringed-instrument playing. Things are only in tune if they sound in tune. The ear alone can identify pitch on the strings.

The same process is now repeated with the D string. The teacher tells the children that the first string was the A string and this second string is the D. "The A is the higher pitched sound on the violins, violas, and cellos, but the lower sound on the basses." The class sings these pitches several times calling them by name. They are shown on the staff on the blackboard in the various clefs.

To continue this pitch identification by ear, the teacher now says, "Listen carefully. I shall pluck a little tune using just these two strings. If you think you can repeat it on your own instrument, raise your hand after you have heard it." The teacher plucks A A A D. Several hands shoot up instantly. After these youngsters have successfully reiterated the notes, the whole class is requested to do so. All then sing the notes calling them by name. The process is repeated with several more motifs as given below:

(1) D D D A D   (2) D A D D A   (3) A D A A D D
(4) D A A D D A A   (5) D D D A A D D   (6) D A D A D A A D

The teacher asks if there is someone in the class who can "make up a tune using only these two strings." One child responds, then he calls on another youngster to repeat his tune. The whole class plays it together and then the second child is given a chance to create a motif, calling on a third child to repeat it. Such a game is continued until the children show complete familiarity with this initial instruction and until the children show by their attitudes that it is time to progress to something more interesting.

Note: The teacher's plucking has been in a steady quarter-note rhythm. When the youngsters take over with their original ideas, rhythmic variations may enter the picture.

Now the teacher plucks another motif in evenly spaced quarter notes: D D D D D D D D A. Here the children find that they have to count in order to know how many D's to play. Rhythmic counting has been subtly introduced. This establishes a rudimentary feeling for the constant reiteration of the regular pulse of music. Thus in the first ten minutes of the class the two most basic elements of music have been touched upon: (1) using the ears to identify pitch and (2) counting time, establishing the feeling for the rhythmic reiteration of the beat. Added to these two fundamentals the creative aspect has been injected--using music to express one's own ideas. The early awakening of the imagination is important, for in its furthest reaches it ultimately supplies musical interpretation. Good teaching methods keep all of these things growing from this time on.

Here it should be stated that there is one essential difference between class methodology and that of the private lesson. In the latter it is oftentimes sufficient to say to the child, "Do it this way." But in good class methodology there must be a series of small, logical steps that will lead everyone in the class from here to there without losing any of them along the way. Each bit of technique has to be built up from an easy starting point, well-known to the child, to arrive in a few minutes at an understanding of the new thing that is being taught. One cannot skip steps in the process when one is dealing with a large group.

Note: We shall now take up the setting of the left hand for each of the four instruments. In the class situation it saves time if the teacher starts with the basses and cellos since they have need for a preliminary exercise which they can practice while the teacher instructs the violins and violas. However, in this book, we shall always present the methodology in the following order: violin-viola, cello, bass.

SETTING THE LEFT HAND: VIOLIN-VIOLA

The students now take the neck of the instrument in the left hand, the strings turned away from the player, and set it in mandolin (or guitar, if you prefer) position.

We now proceed to establish a "feel" for the position of the left hand on the neck of the instrument. The hand is extended (Fig. 1-2), fingers together, little finger directly toward the floor, thumb pointing straight up a kind of "shake hands" position. The end of the neck of the instrument is placed on the first finger just forward of the big base knuckle, at a point that is *opposite* the web that connects the first finger to the second (Fig. 1-3). The youngster should be cautioned not to let the violin ride up to the middle joint of the first finger (Fig. 1-4). When it does so, the fingers cannot fall accurately in tune on the strings, nor can they slide forward and backward to adjust pitch. Such a position often causes youngsters (who may have fundamentally good ears for pitch) to play out of tune, simply because the hand is not in a functionable position.

The thumb now falls into a natural position (forward) an inch to an inch and a half from the end of the neck. The important thing is that its position be natural to the hand in question. Flipping it on and off the neck several times quickly will usually give a cue as to what is natural (Figs. 1-3, 1-5). This forward position of the thumb sets a straight wrist whereas pulling the thumb back, at this time, to the end of the neck, often causes the wrist to collapse into a faulty position.

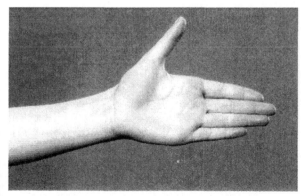

Figure 1-2. The "shake hands" position.

Figure 1-3. Hand placed on neck of violin.

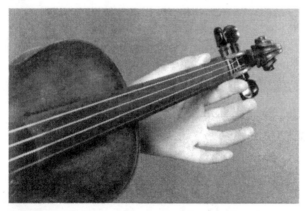

Figure 1-4. Faulty placing of hand on neck of violin.

Figure 1-5. Correct placing of fingers on strings of violin.

Note: The natural function of the thumb is to work in opposition to the fingers so that the hand can grasp things. When the hand hangs completely relaxed, the thumb does not line up parallel with the fingers, but *opposite* to them. This natural, forward position of the thumb should be utilized in the beginning stages of instruction. The length of the individual thumb and its positioning on the individual hand (some thumbs are set higher, some lower on the palm) will determine its ultimate position on the neck of the instrument. A short thumb, set low on the hand, will go more under the neck in playing position. A long thumb, set high on the hand will naturally project above the level of the fingerboard. The teacher must take these things into intelligent consideration in helping individual students to find a comfortable as well as a technically facile setting of the left hand. *After* the wrist has acquired the habit of its good, straight alignment with the arm, the thumb will almost invariably seek out a position closer to the scroll end of the neck. But this should not be permitted to happen if the wrist still collapses. To straighten the wrist, push the thumb forward. In all of this discussion the really important thing is the *fingers, for they play the notes.* Having set the fingers in workable position, the thumb should *accommodate itself to them,* not they to a theoretical approach to the thumb.

The first and second fingers contact the string on the part of the tip of the finger that is closest to the thumb. They form three sides of an approximate square as they fall on the strings and they should *point toward the bridge* (Fig. 1-5). When the violin is raised into playing position, there will be more of the fingertip toward the E string side and the string itself will appear to emerge from under the *center* of the tip of the nail.[2]

Figure 1-6 shows the tendency of the palm of hand to close up toward the neck of the instrument. When this is allowed to happen it forces the fingertip too far over the string (toward the D string), the fingers no longer point toward the bridge, and a collapsed wrist begins to form. The little finger should retain

Figure 1-6. Little finger curving toward fingerboard causing faulty position of fingers on string.

[2]Ivan Galamian, *Principles of Violin Playing and Teaching*, 2/E, © 1985, pp. 15-17. Reprinted by permission of Prentice-Hall, Inc., Englewood Cliffs, New Jersey.

its "toward the floor" position when playing in mandolin style. Compare Fig. 1-6 with Fig. 1-5. It is imperative that the fingertips *point toward the bridge.* Only then do the extension muscles function easily.

Three motions are necessary to the fingers of the left hand: (1) going on and off the strings, (2) moving forward and backward on the string, and (3) slipping directly across from one string to another. Violins, violas, and cellos use all three motions. The string bass uses only the first and third of these motions until such time as the thumb position is needed (seventh position).

It is wise to have the youngsters isolate these motions and practice each one silently just to get the fingers to move easily. There has been perhaps too much emphasis in our beginning methods on habit formation and not enough emphasis on flexibility. We have oftentimes over-conscientiously drilled the youngsters into rigidity, but stringed instrument technique is based on flexibility and we should see that the children experience it right from the very beginning.

The importance of the correct setting of the hand, the correct point of contact of the fingertips on the strings, and the ability to move and adjust the fingers cannot be overemphasized. All of these steps should be reviewed many times during the first year of instruction.

The D major approach is the most natural for the hand--a whole step from first to second finger, a half step from second to third--since it follows the natural construction of the hand. Starting from this point, the extensions are gradually introduced. (See Chapter 4, page 49.) It should be emphasized in the beginning that there are only two possible positions for the fingers on the string--either they are approximately an inch apart (a full inch of vacant space between the fingers) or they *touch* each other on the string. The concept of a "half-inch" is fallacious and should never be mentioned.

CELLO

The first rule is "Sit on the front edge of the chair." Adjust the height of the endpin so that the upper bout of the instrument rests about midway of the child's chest. The right knee straddles the cello in the neighborhood of the circle cut-out on the lower rib of the instrument and the left knee fits near the lower point of the left cut-out. These things are approximate since every measurement of the player's body (length of leg from foot to knee, from knee to thigh, length of torso, and so on) must be comfortably adjusted to the instrument. For this reason it is difficult to be precise. The neck of the instrument should not touch the left shoulder. The C peg is, in height, about level with the player's left ear.

The left arm should form a straight line from elbow to fingers when the hand is in playing position. A trick that helps is as follows: Place the palm of the left hand on the strings at the bridge-end of the finger board (Fig. 1-7) and slide

Figure 1-7. Cello hand at bridge end of fingerboard.

Figure 1-8. Cello hand sliding up to playing position.

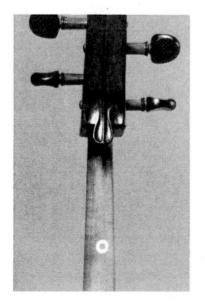

Figure 1-9. Cello neck marked for positioning the thumb

the hand up to playing position (Fig. 1-8). Slip the thumb under the neck of the instrument and curve the fingers, placing them on the D string. The sliding of the hand on its palm up the string as described often helps the arm to assume a natural position as the elbow bends and helps to eliminate the bad curve in the left wrist which either too high or too low an elbow will produce.

The ball of the thumb contacts the back of the neck of the cello *opposite second finger* when that finger is on F natural on the D string. It is helpful if the teacher will outline this position for the thumb as shown in Fig. 1-9. This prevents the thumb from pointing upwards or from getting too far around the neck, either of which positions will prevent the fingers from attaining good action on the strings.

STRING BASS

Have the student stand on the E string side of the bass, facing the rib, with the instrument approximately a foot away from him (Fig. 1-10).

The bass is then leaned over to contact his thigh, and the left knee is placed against the bass on the back of the lower bout (Fig. 1-11)

Note: There are several acceptable positions for the left foot and knee. The one given here seems to be practical for the beginner. In some schools of advanced playing, the left knee does not contact the bass at all.

This point of contact of the knee on the bass is very helpful at first. The student's first lesson is to "balance" the bass, to get it to stand alone without the player's hands touching it. This is a necessary skill since the left hand cannot function freely if it is also trying to support the weight of the bass.

The position of the thumb on the neck of the instrument is similar to that for the cello; in half-position the thumb is opposite second finger when that finger is on E-natural on the D string; in first position, opposite F-natural on the D string. Fig. 1-12 shows both markings.

Figure 1-10. Stance at the side of the string bass.

Figure 1-11. Placing of the knee on the back of the bass. (German Bow)

Figure 1-11b. Seated position with knee in the back of the bass. (French Bow)

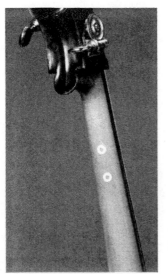

Figure 1-12. Bass neck marked for thum in half and in first position.

If the bass is to correlate with the other instruments in the D-major approach, it will have to start in the first position. When the bass is taught individually or in a homogeneous class, it is better to start with the half position. Notice that in moving the hand from half to first position, the thumb drops approximately two inches down the neck.

THE PRELIMINARY EXERCISE FOR CELLO AND BASS

The importance of the following preliminary study for cello and bass cannot be overemphasized. It produces a good left hand position right from the start and will save time in building that hand's technique. It should be required that the cellos and basses perform well these actions before they join in the D-major scale approach which follows shortly.

After the students have correctly placed the thumb and second finger (basses in first position to correlate with the cellos), the other fingers are dropped on the string. In the cello each finger has approximately an inch of vacant space between itself and the neighboring fingers. On the bass, first to second finger is about a two-inch stretch and second to fourth is another two inches. The bass does not use the third finger for playing notes in the lower positions (I through VI). This finger is first used on the octave harmonic half way down the string's length. However, the third finger should fall onto the string whenever the fourth finger drops into place. Arch all fingers; straighten the arm.

For the sake of quick correlation, use the D string on both instruments. After the initial hand position is set, have the basses slip their four fingers straight across to the G string. The exercise now proceeds: All four fingers ON the string, all four fingers OFF the string, raising just barely off and retaining their stretched position so that when they go back on the string they return to the same relative position. Pluck 4 0 4 0 4 0 4 0 many times. The notes sounded will be G and D on the cello and B-natural (first position) and G on the bass-all part of the G-major chord.

Notice that the tendency during the reiteration will be for the cellos to drop the fingers gradually *down* the neck of the instrument until the first finger (instead of the second finger) is opposite the thumb. On the bass, the fingers will gradually lose their spacing and soon all four will be touching each other on the string. Call attention to these errors and insist that they be avoided. Also, check on the *side* of the first finger. It should be entirely free of the neck, not clinging to the side of the latter. When the fingers are off the string, only the tip of the thumb contacts the neck of the instrument. If allowed to go unchecked, this clinging can develop into a very bad habit, especially on bass, preventing a facile technique and good intonation from developing.

If the teacher will start the class by setting up this study for the cellos and basses first, these students can practice this mechanic silently while the teacher turns her attention to the violins and violas and the correct placing of their hands in the mandolin position. Thereafter all students can pluck their notes together, cellos and basses sounding the 4-0 notes and violins and violas alternating the open D with first finger on the A string (B-natural).

The class may now proceed as a unit on the following studies:

CORRELATING ALL FOUR INSTRUMENTS

Basses slip the fingers over to the A string. All students pluck A A A A, then set the first finger on B and pluck B B B B, A A A A, B B B B, and repeat many times. When this is easy the C-sharp may be added. Cellos will use third finger on the A string, dropping the second finger on the string as the third is placed. Basses will use fourth finger on the A string, dropping the second and third simultaneously. Thus:

A A A A   B B B B   C-sharp   C-sharp   C-sharp   C-sharp

Finally the D is added, basses plucking open D and cellos adding fourth finger; violins and violas place the third finger *close* to the second finger. Be sure the second finger is high enough in pitch.

Transferring all of this to the D string, the foundation is laid for the D-major scale which gradually takes form. (Music Example 1-1 gives the accommodation for the basses without requiring them to shift positions.)

Music Example 1-1.

Having the cellos and basses pluck a descending scale while the violins and violas ascend is also excellent since it starts the low instruments with all four fingers on the string and helps to build a better hand position (Music Example 1-2)

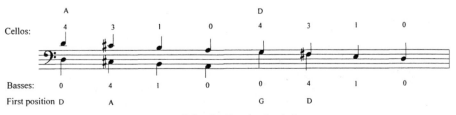

Music Example 1-2.

Do not try to keep this scale moving at a rhythmic pace. Give the youngsters time, every time a new finger is needed, to place it correctly, with perfect position in the hand, before plucking the four rhythmic notes for that finger. Plucking and playing in fours at the beginning is fine because it gives time to adjust pitch before going on to the next note. The pitch should be good by the fourth reiteration of each note.

If there is any time left, the first strain of "Twinkle, Twinkle, Little Star" may be plucked:

		D
Violins-Violas:	D D A A 1 1 <u>A</u>	3 3 2 2 1 1 <u>D</u>
		D
Cellos:	D D A A 1 1 <u>A</u>	4 4 3 3 1 1 <u>D</u>
	G	D
Basses:	D D 1 1 4 4<u>1</u>	G G 4 4 1 1 <u>D</u> (all in first position)

THE SECOND LESSON

The teacher tunes one violin and adjusts it on the child's shoulder. The child's left hand grasps the violin as shown in Fig. 1-13. This position of the left hand is used also during all stages of the beginning bowing. The youngster is now shown how to pluck the string in playing position, the thumb along the side

Figure 1-13. Violin in playing position, preliminary to bowing.

of the fingerboard and the first finger functioning as the plectrum. This child plucks rhythmically his A string while the teacher repeats the process with the next youngster. Each child adds his note to the ensemble as the teacher proceeds around the class tuning the instruments. In this way the tuning period has served to give the youngsters personal attention in addition to getting the instruments in tune. Cellos and basses pluck with the first or the first two fingers of the right hand, the thumb placed along the side of the fingerboard on the lowest-string side. See that the string is pulled sideways, not perpendicularly to the fingerboard, and that all students pluck over the fingerboard, not where the bow plays.

The bows are taken from the cases and laid on the shelf of the music stand, hair down, frog to the right.

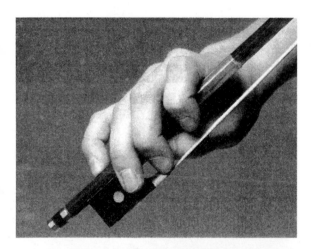

Figure 1-14. Violin bow hand.

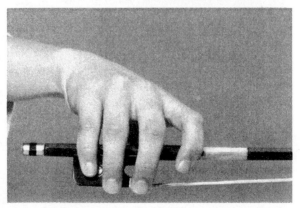

Figure 1-15. Cello bow hand.

Figure 1-16. Bass bow hand (French bow).

HOLDING THE BOW, CORRELATION OF METHOD

The following procedure applies to all four instruments if the bass player is using the French (narrow frog) bow. A circle is formed with the tip of the right thumb and the middle finger, the thumb contacting the finger *beneath the knuckle closest to the nail.* See that the thumb curves outward slightly at its joint. The point of contact is then spread open just far enough to insert the stick of the bow. (The bow is still lying on the music stand.) On all four bows, the thumb contacts the stick *next to the frog but not in the frog.* For the violin and viola bow, the thumb will be slightly more *under* the stick than on the cello and bass bows. It must never stick out on the far side of the bow.

Note: The small cut-out in the frog fascinates youngsters. It looks so much as if it were made just to accommodate a little thumb-tip. Placing the thumb in the cut-out prevents both its needed curve (violin and viola) and its future flexibility. Children should be told that the cut-out exists *only* for the purpose of rehairing the bow — the little silver slide slips off the lower projection.

The first finger may now be dropped onto the stick, contacting the bow between the middle and tip-joint of that finger, and on cello and bass spreading a bit farther away from the thumb. Refer to Figs. 1-14 (violin-viola), 1-15 (cello), and 1-16 (bass).

The ring finger goes well over the stick onto the far side of the frog. On violin and viola it may come to rest on the pearl dot or near it, and the little finger will be placed on top of the stick, close enough to the ring finger to curve slightly. Under no circumstances must this small finger be stretched out toward the end of the stick, becoming stiff and straight. On the cello and bass, the ring finger reaches farther over the frog, coming almost to the bottom of the frog, and the little finger also reaches over, aligning itself next to the ring finger with its tip above the pearl dot or directly upon the dot (depending upon the relative length of these last two fingers).

It is good to stress "sponginess" in the base knuckles of the bow-hand fingers, especially for the violinists and violists. One can press on these knuckles and teach them to collapse. Curving the little finger will eliminate its stiffness. Children invariably grip the bow too tightly complaining, "I'm afraid I'll drop it."

If the wide-frog German bow is used by the basses, the player may proceed as follows: Hang the bow point downward, stick to the left of the hair; place the

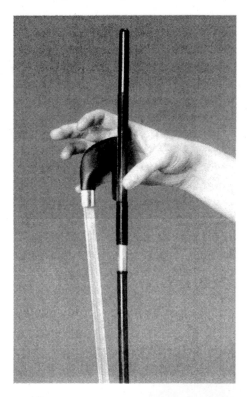

Figure 1-17.
Preliminary position
for the German bass
bow.

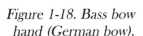

Figure 1-18. Bass bow
hand (German bow).

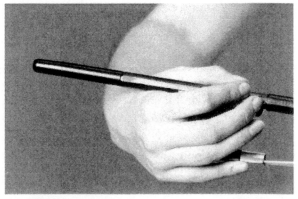

right thumb on the stick above the frog and the little finger beneath the frog (Fig. 1-17). Then flip the bow into its horizontal playing position (Fig. 1-18). The long extension of the stick contacts the side of the first finger. The tips of the first and second fingers contact the stick on the far side of the frog and the ring finger is inserted slightly into the cut-out.

STARTING THE TONE

When all bow hands have been set correctly and the process reviewed several times, the instruments are placed in playing position, the bow is lifted from the music stand and set on the strings half way between bridge and fingerboard, ready for the first tones. The violins and violas will set the bow about at its middle; the cellos and basses set it at the frog. It should be stressed for the violins and violas that the *strings support the bow,* and the bow-hand need only guide it. All students now proceed to play short bows, *down-bow, up-bow.* Cello and bass bows rest on the *inner edge of the hair* — violin and viola bows rest on the full surface of the hair.

A short period of "free practice" is good now. No effort is made to "keep the class together." During this period of experimentation, the teacher circulates making corrections where necessary and giving needed individual help. This "free practice" device is excellent whenever a new piece of technique is presented for the first time.

Throughout all of the bowing practice, stress should be laid on keeping the bow parallel with the bridge--like two railroad tracks--or in making a "good square corner" at the point where the bow contacts the string, and preserving that "square corner" throughout the stroke.

Cellos and basses should be taught the press-release-play approach for their initial attempts with the bow. Set the bow on the string at the frog and depress the string by adding pressure to the bow. (This pressure gets the entire length of these long strings under the control of the bow.) The pressure is then released and, simultaneously with the release, the motion of the bow-stroke starts. This guarantees a better "bass" quality in the resulting tone.

THE BOW ARM AND HAND: VIOLIN-VIOLA

When the bow is resting on the string half way down the bow's length, the arm will form a right-angle at the elbow and the wrist is flat. Conversely when this angle forms and the wrist is flat, the bow is at its half-way point *in relation to that student's individual arm length.* This is an important point. Off-the-string bowings (spiccato) will come between this point and the frog; on-the-string bowings (short détaché) will come at this point or between it and the tip, generally speaking. Also, the motion of the whole-bow stroke changes as this mid-point is passed. More of this later on. This is called the "square" position of the bow arm. See Fig. 2-2, page 23. As the bow approaches the point, the right elbow pushes gradually forward to preserve the straight bow-stroke.

CELLO

The bow hangs down from a gently curved wrist as it contacts the string at the frog. The inner edge of the hair is on the string and the stick is top-side of the hair.

BASS

The bass player's bow-arm should hang down straight from the shoulder without any ungainly bend in the elbow. If the height of the bass is too tall for the individual player, he will have to bend his elbow in order to set the bow at the proper place of contact on the strings. (Refer to page 2.)

CONCLUDING THE SECOND LESSON

The setting of the bow hand should be drilled many times during this class, starting with the initial forming of the circle of thumb and middle finger. After the free practice period, the teacher may set a beat and bring the class together into a good and synchronized rendition of quarter notes on the open strings: violins-violas moving from middle toward the point on the down-bow, cellos-basses moving from the frog toward the middle.

The class may now play four A's, stop, lean the bow over to the D string, play four D's, stop, tip the bow back onto the A string, and so on. The teacher controls the length of the stop until all bows are correctly set on the new string each time. The four notes are played rhythmically, with good ensemble. The bows are not lifted from the string in making the crossing but are simply tilted over from one string to the next.

After this introductory work with the bow, the teacher should review the plucking exercises in mandolin position, if he has used them in a preceding lesson.

CHAPTER TWO
THE NEXT EIGHT LESSONS

O ne should be flexible in the application of the following outlines. Some classes move faster, some slower. There should be no pressure at this stage to accomplish everything as stated in each lesson. The important thing is to have a logical sequence in the instruction and to continue in the following lesson the work completed in the previous class. The teacher should neither skip nor neglect any of these beginning steps but should see that the instruction is thouroughly understood and adequately performed before proceeding.

THE THIRD LESSON

The tuning period should also contribute to the forward progress of the class. In this third lesson the teacher tunes the first instrument, helps the child to adjust it correctly into playing position (Fig. 1-13), checks the bow hand for a good easy position on the stick, and has the child start bowing the A string with short bows in the middle of the bow (violin), as set forth in Lesson Two. Each child in turn adds his A-string bowing to the ensemble as the teacher proceeds around the class giving this individual attention. The teacher should not spend any great amount of time with any one youngster but should work rapidly and efficiently. This proceeding may take longer than a mere tuning process, but it produces effective results. The children are practicing instead of sitting idly by, and they appreciate having individualized instruction from the teacher.

Note: The goals for the next eight lessons are: gradual development of the whole-bow stroke, increasing skill in the D-major scale, the use of the bow and fingers simultaneously, and acquiring the ability to play at least one tune nicely (by rote) with bow and fingers. Flexibility of the muscular structure, not rigidity, should eventuate.

On all of the instruments, if the left hand tires, it is probably excessive pressure of the thumb that is causing the trouble. Flipping the thumb off and instantly replacing it, while playing, is helpful, and gradually eliminates the clutching.

DEVELOPMENT OF THE BOW-STROKE

On the violin and viola it has been found most effective to develop the bow-stroke first from the middle to the point before going to the frog. (This statement is the result of many years of experimentation with both methods.) When the novice begins by using the bow first at the frog, there is almost invariably a shrugged right shoulder. This shrugging is a subtle fault in that it some-

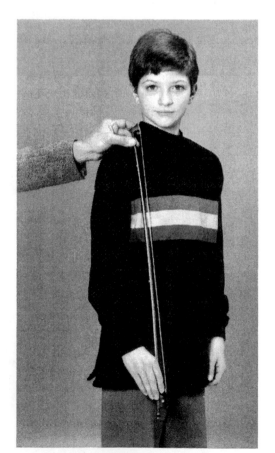

Figure 2-1. Measuring the violin bow for proper length.

Figure 2-2. Violin and bow in standing playing position.

Figure 2-2b. Violin and bow in seated playing position.

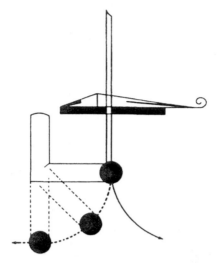

Figure 2-3. Diagram depicting the path of the bow stroke: violin.

times remains undetected for years. It can be the cause of many related diffi-culties. When the bowing moves first from the middle to the point, the forward reach (needed to keep the bow straight near the tip) pulls the shoulder down and lessens the tendency to shrug when, later on, the frog end of the bow is introduced. (This is particularly true in college-level classes of beginners.)

Setting the bow at its mid-point, move the stroke as far toward the tip of the bow as the length of the arm will permit without letting that arm swing back-ward in order to go all the way to the end of the bow. In cases where the bow is too long for the child's arm, a marker should be placed on the stick several inches from the point and the youngster warned not to go past that mark. "For you, this is the 'end of the bow.' " See Figure 2-1 as a guide to measuring the bow's length in relation to the child's arm.

In drawing the stroke from the middle to the point, the child learns to push gradually forward with the elbow and upper arm as the point is approached on the down-bow. This helps to keep the bow at right angles to the string. (Such a motion is also pertinent to the cello when bowing on the A string.)

As the up-bow starts, the elbow and upper arm move gently backward, can-celing out the forward reach. The right angle in the elbow forms again as the middle of the bow is reached (Fig. 2-2).

Since all motions of the arms are naturally circular in character (the motion originating always from a joint which becomes the center of a circle), the result-ing natural arc has to be counteracted when straight-line motion is desired (Fig. 2-3).

The dotted line shows the natural arc-like motion of the arm as it simply opens up from the elbow. The solid arrows show the accommodation the arm must make in order to keep the bow moving in a straight line. The amount of accommodation necessary depends entirely upon the length of the individual arm in relation to the bow's static length.

After the section from the middle to the point has been developed with good straightness and flexibility, the middle to frog section may be introduced. As the bow approaches the frog, going up-bow, the stick gradually rolls over toward the scroll and the *outer edge of the bow hair* contacts the string instead of the full surface. At the very frog, the tip of the bow will *point forward.* This tilting accomplishes three things: (1) it removes some of the bow-hair from the string so that the pressure at the frog is released a bit, thus making for a better sound; (2) it starts the development of the wrist flexibility, for the wrist bends as the bow rolls toward the outer edge of the hair; and (3) it straightens the bow at the frog. When the youngsters arrive at the frog with full hair surface contacting the string, the bow usually points over the left shoulder, crookedly. Also, the wrist acquires a tendency to turn inward toward the player's chin which is a bad fault. When there are three good reasons for a piece of *beginning* technique, it is well to give it special attention. Wrist flexibility should be built right from the beginning. This section of the bow is used in Lesson Eight.

In progressing from the frog to the middle, starting on the outer edge of the hair, the bow-stick gradually resumes its position perpendicularly above the hair with the full hair surface on the string. This rolling motion, done without exaggeration, makes for a natural flexibility in the wrist. Bending the thumb-joint outward is particularly helpful in loosening the wrist muscles. A curved-in, rigid thumb tightens a big muscle in the wrist.

On cello and bass, the frog of the bow is the easier section for the beginner to use. The players of these instruments, therefore, should be developing the lower half of the bow while the violins and violas are working with the upper half. Cellos and basses should play on the inner edge of the hair throughout their stroke. As pressure is added, more of the hair-surface contacts the string. Basses should pay attention to keeping the tip of the bow pointed upward. If the tip of the bow slants toward the floor, it gives a crooked stroke on the string, since the bass is at an angle as it leans toward the player.

EXERCISES FOR THE ENTIRE CLASS

Violins and violas use the bow from the middle to the point, cellos and basses from the frog to the middle in the following studies.

1. D, D: down-bow, up-bow. Stop after every pair of notes and check the bow for straightness. Basses, see that the bow is pointing upward when at the frog. Repeat many times.
2. A, A: same procedure as (1).
3. Alternate: D, D. Stop and set the bow on the A string. Play A, A. Stop and set the bow on the D string. The setting of the bow on the new

string is done without lifting it from the strings. Just tilt it over to the new string each time. Repeat many times.

4. D, D, A, A. Stop. Then A, A, D, D. When this manner of execution has become easy, the stop may be eliminated. Make the stop long enough so that each child can plan definitely what he is going to do next. Stop also before repeating the exercise.

5. Start at the middle of the bow on cello and bass and at the point of the bow on violin and viola. Set the bow straight across the string (a good, square-corner at the point of contact of hair and string). Repeat exercises (1) through (4), using the up-bow, down-bow stroke. Check the bow for straightness during each stop.

6. For review, use Music Example 2-1, stressing good position of the left hand on cello and bass.

Initial plucking study, particularly important for the cellos and basses.

*To simplify, substitute the small notes.

Homogeneous class of basses $^{1}/_{2}$ position

Music Example 2-1.

7.   Pluck "Twinkle, Twinkle, Little Star."

THE FOURTH LESSON

During tuning period. Check the bow-hand of each student after tuning his instrument and have him start bowing after the manner of the preceding lesson. Use the A string. (Start the tuning with a different child each time so that the longest period of playing is gradually passed around.)

Review the bowing exercises of Lesson Three.

Review the plucking exercises of Lessons One and Three.

Add this new facet of rhythmic plucking: Take the name of a child in the class, spoken rhythmically, and pluck the open string in this rhythm, as given in Music Example 2-2.[1]

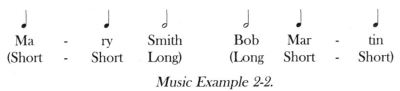

Ma	-	ry	Smith	Bob	Mar	-	tin
(Short	-	Short	Long)	(Long	Short	-	Short)

Music Example 2-2.

Setting the instruments into playing position, the rhythms may then be bowed.

THE FIFTH LESSON

During tuning period. Bowing from the middle to the point on violin and viola, and from frog to middle on cello and bass, keeping the bow straight. A string.

Bow the rhythms of the names in Lesson Four using the A string some of the time and the D string part of the time.

Have the violins and violas set the left hand in mandolin position (left wrist straight, thumb forward). Then, with the help of the right hand, raise the instruments into playing position, the left hand remaining as set. All students pluck the D scale in playing position, four plucks to each note, ascending and descending. (See Music Example 1-1 for the string bass fingering.)

Here an effective trick for the violin and viola may be used. Draw an ink line on the fingernails of the left hand, starting in the center of the nail and proceeding downward to the very center of the nail's tip. Have the children place the ink line directly above the string at the point of contact. This helps in set-

[1]The author first saw this technique used in a demonstration of rhythms for the elementary school given by Mary Jarman Nelson. The idea is fully developed in the book *Rhythms Today!* by Edna Doll and Mary Jarman Nelson. ©1965 Silver Burdett Company. Used by permission.

ting a good position for the fingers in relation to the string. Mark only first and second fingers.

For plucking in playing position, see that the upper strings have the thumb of the right hand correctly placed along the *side of the fingerboard* and that they are plucking with the index finger. The setting of the thumb in this manner furnishes a point of resistance for the pulling of the string in the plucking action.

Pluck "Twinkle, Twinkle, Little Star" in playing position.

Note: If the violins and violas have a tendency to collapse the left wrist at this time, see that the thumb is forward, opposite where the second finger would be if it were on F-natural on the D string.[2]

THE SIXTH LESSON

PREPARING FOR READING

By this time the children are getting a feel for the instrument and usually their eyes begin to stray from close observation of their hands. When this happens it is a cue for the teacher to begin training the eyes in a reading process.

Manual habits are not yet firmly enough established to risk having the eyes and mind become fully occupied with reading all of the unfamiliar symbols of the music staff. But they will work effectively at this time on *familiar* symbols. Therefore we introduce the Letter-Number Reading. *Its sole purpose is to get the eyes to function away from the instrument.*

Write the following symbols on the blackboard:

Violins:		Basses:	G
Violas:	D D A A 1 1 <u>A</u>	First position	D D 1 1 4 4 <u>1</u>
Cellos:			

		D
Violins:	D	Basses: G G 4 4 1 1 <u>D</u>
Violas:	3 3 2 2 1 1 <u>D</u>	

	D
Cellos:	4 4 3 3 1 1 <u>D</u>

The string named is plucked as an open string. The number tells what finger to place *on that string* for the next note. When the melody requires that the fin-

---

[2]Leopold Auer states: "Try to hold the thumb thrust forward more in the direction of the second and third fingers," and again, speaking of F-natural on the D string, "the thumb is directly opposite." *Violin Playing as I Teach it* (New York: J. B. Lippincott Co., 1921,1949), p.34. Galamian also agrees with the forward position of the thumb.

ger be placed on a different string, the new string is notated *above* the required finger. A long line under a letter or number signifies a long note. The fewest possible symbols to get the idea across are the most effective.

In letter-number reading, the open strings and first fingers are the same for all instruments (basses in first position). But above the first finger the cellos have to "add a number." (Second finger on violin and viola will require third finger on cello.) The basses have to add two numbers. For example, where violins play second finger (key of D major, D and A strings only), the basses must play fourth finger (for F-sharp and C-sharp). Teaching the children this quick addition trick will save time since writing one set of symbols on the board will suffice.

Note: If the violins play three fingers, the basses, adding two, will get five. This means by-passing the fourth finger and going over to the next open string.

When the children come in for their sixth lesson, they find the following letters and numbers on the blackboard:

(1) D D A A 1 1 <u>A</u> $\overset{\text{D}}{3}$ 3 2 2 1 1 <u>D</u>   and repeat
      D   D
  A A 3 3 2 2 <u>1</u>   A A 3 3 2 2 <u>1</u>
Repeat first line here.

(2) (Title)   ?
  D
  2 1 D 1 2 2 <u>2</u>   1 1 <u>1</u>   2 A <u>A</u>
  D
  2 1 D 1 2 2 2 2   1 1 2 1 <u>D</u>

(3) (Title)   ?
  D
  2 2 <u>2</u>   2 2 <u>2</u>   2 A D 1 <u>2</u>
  D
  3 3 3 3   3 2 2 2   2 1 1 2 <u>1</u>   <u>A</u>
Repeat first line, then play this next line:
  D   D
  3 3 3 3   3 2 2 2   A A 3 1   <u>D</u>

Since children are endowed with tremendous curiosity, they will immediately want to know "What is all that stuff on the blackboard?"

The teacher explains how to figure out the letters and numbers and then tells the class to pluck them (free practice) and find out what the tunes are.

Natural curiosity makes the youngsters' eyes work most effectively away from the instrument. An excited smile and dancing eyes accompany the first hand that shoots up when one of the children recognizes the tune.

Note: The teacher can either put the symbols on the board for cello and bass or he can explain the addition of fingers for those instruments, indicating in parentheses the bass fingerings when the skip may be too troublesome. In teaching the winds, this letter-number step is not so important because the approach to reading is inclined to be a note-by-note activity. Reading one note at a time, sequentially, simplifies the initial contact with the reading process and also the winds do not have the exaggerated bi-manual problem of the strings. However, some wind teachers have adapted letter-number reading and have found it useful.

Mimeographed copies of the letter-number tunes are given to the youngsters to take home after class. (Cello and Bass parts should be notated correctly for those instruments.) It is suggested that the students sing the tunes using the letters and numbers. This helps them to associate the fingerings with the pitches, and it can form the first stage of home study. (The reader will remember that it is our stated conviction that no home practice should be permitted until the first ten lessons are completed satisfactorily under class supervision.)

After plucking such tunes becomes easy, using the fingers and bow together may begin. The first finger on the D string is bowed, then the second finger (violin-viola), third finger (cello), fourth finger (bass). Each finger is isolated and worked on separately. Finally the D-major scale emerges, bowed four times on each note.

THE SEVENTH LESSON

During tuning period. Bowing, alternating two A's with two D's.

Letter-number reading is reviewed, plucking in playing position. Watch for straight wrists in the violins, violas, and cellos and basses. Do not let the cellos and bass left arms sag so that there is a sharp curve in the wrist. This interferes with the facile use of the fingers.

The D scale is bowed, four bows per note. Stop at the end of each group of four and set the next finger before testing it for pitch. Emphasize that if the finger is out of tune on the first bowed stroke, the student should adjust its position on the string and try to get it in tune before the last of the four bows is played. At this point, individual help in how to adjust (whether to move the finger up or down) is imperative. Scatter such help throughout the lesson period, but see that all youngsters understand how to make the adjustments. Going back to the very first lesson, drill the sliding motions of the fingers (silently) as suggested there (page 8).

The scale is now played without the stops. Then the rhythm of a child's name is superimposed as given in Lesson Four.

Play "Twinkle, Twinkle, Little Star" with the bow.

THE EIGHTH LESSON

During tuning period. The A string is bowed. Violins, violas start at the point and go up to the middle, returning to the point on the down-bow. A stop is made at the tip of the bow and the child checks his bow for straightness at the point of contact with the string. Cellos and basses start in the middle of the bow and go to the frog, checking for straightness throughout the stroke. By this time the youngsters have become accustomed to the tuning routines and the teacher can take a minute, before starting to tune, to explain to the whole group what the "tuning trick" for the day will be. Today it is a "free practice" routine, each child moving at his own speed.

This lesson deals with the presentation of the "other half of the bow." Violins and violas will now go to the frog, cellos and basses move from the middle to the point. Violins and violas should roll the stick over toward the scroll as the frog is approached. Cellos and basses should use whatever forward reach is necessary to keep the bow straight at the point. A slight traveling toward the bridge is not bad (provided pressure is added thereto) since it forms part of the cello-bass technique for sustained tones later on (page 74).

The D scale can now be bowed using this section of the bow, still four bows per note.

The plucking of tunes is reviewed in playing position. Bowing is added where feasible. Children can begin to "solo," as a final requirement for taking the instruments home for the first time. When a child can play presentably "Twinkle, Twinkle, Little Star" with the bow, he is ready to start home practice- and to have his parents hear him for the first time.

THE NINTH LESSON

A complete review of everything, from the very first steps, should now be given. This will take most of the period. Solo performances may be continued.

THE TENTH LESSON

During tuning period. Bowing on the lower half of the bow for violins and violas, upper half for cellos and basses.

Information on how to take care of the instruments is presented. Lay stress on two things: (1) "Do not lay your case down so that the violin is resting on its bridge. Always see that the case is right side up." (2) **"Never turn your back on**

an unlocked case, even for a moment. If you are practicing at home and the phone rings or Mother calls you to do something, lay the instrument in its case and flip the lock before you leave. Many accidents happen and instruments get broken because that lock has not been fastened shut. While you are gone you may forget your case is unlocked and later, when you hurriedly pick it up, out falls the violin. Or someone else may come into the room and pick it up to move it, with the same unhappy result. Repairs cost from $25.00 to $100.00 if you break the instrument. So save yourself that expense and heartbreak by flipping that lock before you turn your back."

Note: In teaching violin as a secondary instrument on the college level, the vibrato motion is usually started about this time-just the motion itself. It comes easier for the adult student if it is begun before the hand freezes into a permanent position on the instrument (pages 73-74).

Upon the completion of these first ten lessons, the class is usually ready to take up serious study of music reading and to step across into a lesson book, proceeding according to its directions. Home practice is initiated. Classes should meet *twice a week* during the balance of the year.

GENERAL GOALS FOR THE YEAR'S WORK

The first year's development deals with the following problems:

1. Getting the ear to hear pitch and to know which way to move a finger to play perfectly in tune. (Sing the faulty pitch and then see which way the voice has to slide in order to get the note in tune.)

2. Keeping the fingers down on the strings as much as possible. Do not let them fly off into the air. They need not press heavily when not actually playing a note, but they should rest on the strings whenever possible. When the third finger is played, the first and second fingers should be on the string also. When the fourth finger is played, the first, second, and third should fall into position, contacting the string. This applies to all four instruments. When the fingers rest on the strings, the *feel* of good intonation is constantly being acquired by the hand. When they are in the air, they develop only tension. Keep fingers curved.

3. Keeping the fingers close to the strings when they are in the air, off the strings. At the top level of proficiency there is no time to raise the fingers high. The music moves too fast. As much as possible, beginning techniques should tend to develop habits that will be used later on. There are a few exceptions where a beginning habit has to precede the final habit.

4. Building slurred bowing. The best way to introduce slurring is to have the children draw a long, slow bow, and then bounce the first finger on

and off the string as many times as possible before getting to the end of the bow. Later, keep the first finger on and bounce the next finger on and off. This is not only a good finger drill, but it gets the slurring process under way much more easily than does the slow act of slurring only two notes on one bow. The latter should be the second step since it entails more control. Using the many-note approach, the tone may not be quite as vital, but certain beneficial things will happen; for one, it starts the development of the slow-motion stroke from one end of the bow to the other. It is not unusual for youngsters to come back for the next lesson with some forty or fifty notes per bow.

5. Improving constantly the closeness of the half steps. Stress the high pitch of the lower note of the pair and the low pitch of the upper note. Pay attention to the close finger-tip contact (violin and viola) when the two fingers in question are on neighboring strings (minor sixths and augmented fourths).

6. Acquiring some knowledge of and facility in one-octave scales. Also two-octave G and C scales are workable. Basses can repeat the C scale, one-octave form, while the others are playing two octaves. All students can be taught to finger the two-octave G scale, basses included, violas to third position, cellos to fourth. Call the attention of the cellos to the fact that in fourth position the notes that are an octave higher than the corresponding first position notes use exactly the same fingers.

7. Sometimes the vibrato motion is started. This will depend upon the class and the students individually. Some may be ready, some not.

8. Memorizing various tunes which can be played as solos. An excellent volume for this is *Tone Poems for Strings* by Anthony Bacich. It is one of the very few books that provides solos for beginners in unison on all four stringed instruments. After the class session all students have a solo to practice and play.

9. Developing tone quality throughout the entire first year together with a proper use of whole-bow and half-bow strokes.

Regarding memory work and tonal development--the two go hand in hand. After a piece is memorized, tone can be greatly stressed. As for the memorizing, the ear takes care of most of it, but where there is a sudden difficulty the mind must come into play. It must *know* what is causing the difficulty. For example: "The first time you come to this spot the second-finger note is played four times. The next time it happens in the music that note is played only two times and you go on down the scale." The teacher should analyze such things for the beginner so that he can see how to approach his memory work later on. It is usually the note that acts as the switch in the track (the first note that is different in the second reiteration of the melody) that causes the trouble. When that single note is located and set consciously into the mind, then the memorization will proceed with ease and without mishap.

10.   Laying a foundation for future speed and clarity in the left-hand finger-action.

At the turn of the century the philosophy was "lift the fingers high and hit them down hard on the string." The results were tension, a slowing down in the ultimate technique, and, in some cases, the onset of a muscular paralysis in the left hand (known as "violinist's hand") accompanied by a ruined career. Today we substitute the words "clean articulation" for the "thumping down hard" and a close-to-the-string approach instead of a "lifting high" of the fingers. An excellent first study is as follows: Start a long slow-moving bow stroke; then, upon a given signal, drop the first finger suddenly onto the string and get it off again *instantly*. Let it relax as soon as it comes off the string. Repeat this action several times per bow-stroke. When it has become easy, reverse it; start with the finger *on* the string and let it come off and go back on immediately. Repeat the process with each finger. When second finger is activated, first finger should rest constantly on the string in a relaxed manner, and so on.

Some of the material of Chapter 4 will also be found useful in the first year classes. It may be used with students of outstanding aptitude, giving them things to accomplish in their home practice (more rhythms, more bowings) on the "same old scales" as the rest of the class.

FLEXIBILITY FACTORS

Relaxed joints are *curved*. Perfect straightness in a joint means that muscular tension is present. Curve the fingers as they contact the strings (all four instruments). When playing on a lower-pitched string, *arch* the fingers over the upper strings. Press the strings straight down vertically. Unwanted tension exists when a finger pulls the string out of line. Such pulling causes the tip-joint of the finger to collapse inward. Since the finger joints are flexible, see that they "break" outward. Excessive pressure in thumb and fingers builds tension instead of technique. Adding pressure *after* the string contacts the fingerboard is of no value tonally or technically.

Overly conscientious or nervously tense youngsters often "freeze" the bow arm. (1) Relax the shoulder. (2) Gently pull the bow in the down-bow stroke as the child holds it, showing him thereby that he is resisting motion instead of "letting the arm move." An elbow held too high is often the cue that the shoulder is shrugging.

CHAPTER THREE
THE TEACHING OF MUSIC
READING

The teaching of music reading has been made far more complicated than is necessary due to the fact that we are too prone to starting with the end result instead of putting first things first.

THE ESSENCE OF MUSIC READING

Music reading is comprised of three steps: (1) The eyes must see the symbols, (2) the association centers of the brain must interpret those symbols instantly and accurately, and (3) the mind must then send out the message to the corresponding muscles to perform the actions that will result in the musical sounds of a rhythmic nature.

In language reading, each word tells just one thing. But in music reading each symbol tells two things: (1) What pitch to play and (2) how long it is to last. For every sign in music the mind must make two interpretations simultaneously. Too often in teaching music we forget to tell this simple fact to the child. This double concept should be highlighted rather than ignored.

We are given to showing our beginners how to perform the notes and then to proceeding immediately to problems in higher musical mathematics. We expect these novice pupils to do problems in addition and even in fractions before we have given them time to get thoroughly acquainted with whole numbers, which whole numbers are, after all, the basis of the mathematical science.

What we should do is (1) show the students how to perform the indicated pitches; (2) then emphasize the existence of regularly spaced intervals of time (the takt, the basic pulse); and (3) teach them, as a basic habit to group all notes into *units with a duration of one full beat*. When this whole-number approach is thoroughly grasped, it will be time to become scholarly in demanding the splitting of the beat into its precise fractional parts.

To put it another way, let us first teach the eyes (and mind) to *see what makes a beat, i.e., to recognize instantly how much of the music is to be played on each beat. Seeing the total unit of the beat should precede the splitting of that beat into its fractional divisions.*

It is interesting to note that Leopold Mozart, father of Wolfgang Amadeus Mozart, tried, in 1756, to pound this fact into the stubborn minds of the music teachers of his day. To quote:

> Beginners will suffer no little harm if they perpetually count the eighth notes [the "ands"]. How is it possible for a pupil, whom the teacher perplexes with such fallacious teaching, to get on in even a moderately fast tempo if he counts every eighth note? And, what is even worse, if he divides all the half-notes and even whole notes mentally into eighth notes, by making perceptible accents with the bow, and also (as I have heard myself) counts in a loud voice, or even taps so many beats with the foot? People excuse themselves on the grounds that this way of teaching has arisen out of the necessity to accustom the beginner to grasp quickly the proportional division of time. [The same old argument is still being used.] But that kind of habit remains, and the pupil depends on it and finally becomes unable to play one bar correctly without this counting. One must therefore try to instill the quarter notes thoroughly into his mind and then so arrange the instruction that the beginner may be able to divide such quarters into eighths with exactitude, the eighths into sixteenths, and so on.[1]

Perhaps the reason "Papa" Mozart did not succeed in convincing the profession lies in the fact that he did not fully implement his criticism with a positive and spelled-out methodology. We shall, therefore, take up where he left off, with the hope that the twentieth-century pedagogic mind is a little more flexible than its counterpart was in 1756 and thereafter.

Two comments are necessary first. Mozart mentions the foot-tap. The fact that big muscles are already in use rhythmically in the bow-arm eliminates the need for further bodily stress in the form of the foot-tap. Also, since the bimanual problem of the strings requires complicated mental-physical functioning from the youngster, the rhythm has to take second place in importance in the beginning stages. The rhythmic drive has to be upset at times in deference to the correct functioning of the hands. *Correct manual habits should precede correct rhythmic habits.* After all, rhythm is not a god, divine though its properties may be.

The second comment has to do with Mozart's statement: "People excuse themselves on the grounds that this way of teaching has arisen out of the neces-

---

[1] Leopold Mozart, *A Treatise on the Fundamental Principles of Violin Playing*, trans. Editha Knocker (London: Oxford University Press, second edition, 1951, reprinted 1959), p.34. The original translation uses the English designations: minims, crotchets, and so on. These have been changed to the American equivalents in the quotation given herein. Interpolated remarks in brackets are the author's.

sity to accustom the beginner to grasp quickly the proportional division of time."

There is nothing much more illogical than our "proportional division of time." In all mathematics except music, the number "one" signifies the whole unit. We speak of one pie (a whole pie), one instrument (the whole instrument), one nation (the whole nation), one beat (the whole beat). But in music we customarily call the note that signifies one whole beat "a quarter note." A whole note is not unity, "one," but *four* units, four "ones." It is no wonder that musical mathematics confuse the youngster.

Having made these two comments let us proceed with the methodology.

THE UNITY OF THE BEAT

In the second paragraph of this chapter we mentioned a very important step in the reading process; the association centers of the brain must interpret instantly and accurately the meanings of the musical symbols. The first step in gaining security in reading rhythm is to train these association centers through drill to interpret instantly the rhythmic meaning of the individual symbols. Reading rhythm can become an instantaneous reaction. Identical rhythms may be used by different composers, but the minute two composers put the same pitches in the same sequence on the same rhythm, they have the same composition. Where rhythms are identical, the pitches must furnish the variation. Therefore, the thing that must become *automatic* in the reading process is the interpretation of the rhythmic values of the symbols so that the mind is free, in reading new music, to concentrate on the pitches since this is where the variation will take place.

Our first step, then, is to see that the young mind is given sufficient time to acquire facility in interpreting the fundamental rhythmic values of musical symbols.

The teacher can place on the chalkboard the following notations, at random: A quarter note, a half note, a quarter rest, a whole rest, and a half rest; also a *pair* of eighths (not just a single eighth), thus stressing the *unity* rather than the *division* of the beat (Music Example 3-1).

Music Example 3-1.

Notice the terminology for the pair of eighths. The word "partners" further promotes the unifying concept. (See pages 38-41 for the full discussion of basic-concept terminology.)

As the teacher points from one symbol to another, the class counts *the exact value* of that symbol. The counting is done on a strict takt. It is done without interruption, the takt being continuous. After the children have learned to count in this manner the words under the symbols are erased and the process repeated until the mental interpretation of each symbol is instantaneous and accurate. This will take several days of drill.

Now we come to another important reading principle: *Know how much of*

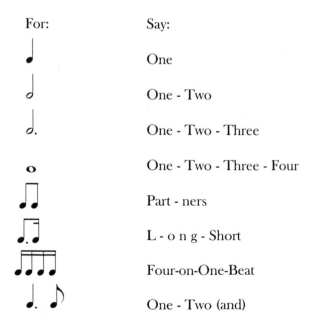

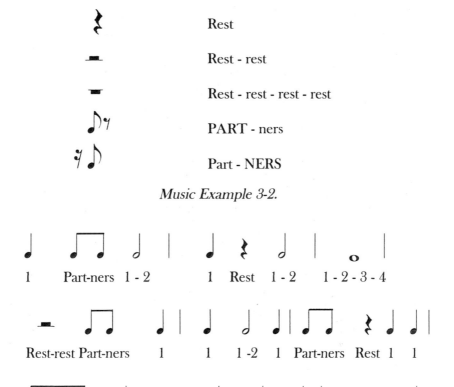

𝄽	Rest
▬	Rest - rest
▬	Rest - rest - rest - rest
♪𝄾	PART - ners
𝄾♪	Part - NERS

Music Example 3-2.

♩   ♫♩   ♩ | ♩   𝄽   ♩ | o |
1   Part-ners 1 - 2   1   Rest   1 - 2   1 - 2 - 3 - 4

▬   ♫♩   ♩ | ♩   ♩   ♩ | ♫♩   𝄽   ♩   ♩ |
Rest-rest Part-ners   1   1   1 -2   1   Part-ners   Rest   1   1

♫   ♩   𝄾   ♪   ♩ | ♩.   𝄽 |
Long - short   1   Part - NERS   1   1 - 2 - 3   Rest

Music Example 3-3.

the music to play on each beat. Our stress is laid on *grouping* everything into the value of one beat, rather than in splitting a beat into smaller units.

We therefore need some special terminology. Each time the child is confronted with one of the following symbols, his mind should interpret it as given in Music Example 3-2.

Applying this to musical rhythm, the youngster will count it as follows, keeping the takt (beat) perfectly even (Music Example 3-3).

In this way the basic concepts that need to be learned first are drilled simply and directly. The association centers of the brain are taught to interpret, instantly and accurately, exactly what the symbols mean, uncluttered by additional problems in mental arithmetic. The minute the "one-two-three-four" counting is introduced, the child's mental processes are encumbered with problems in addition (Music Example 3-4).

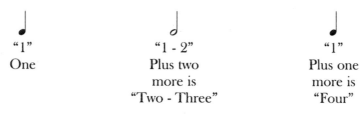

Music Example 3-4.

There is nothing wrong with this way of counting time except that it has been customarily presented as the *first* step when it should follow along in logical sequence as the *second* step. It becomes easily functional only after the basic rhythmic concepts have become second nature. Actually, there is no necessity to add up the beats in the measure until participation in a large ensemble requires that the conductor's beat-patterns be identified with each beat in the bar and that his "One" in each measure be clearly recognized.

Referring to the time-counting chart (Music Example 3-2) it is seen that a pair of eighths is called "partners." Here is an example of what we mean by the "unity of the beat." This word "partners" is so wonderfully rhythmic in its spoken form. The almost-even accenting of the two syllables together with the very slight emphasis on the first syllable, gives the right rhythmic feeling for the correct execution of the two eighths. They are played just as they are spoken. Further, this terminology *groups the two eighths together into one unit,* instead of splitting the unit into its fractional divisions—a subtle but important difference in the eye-mind approach.

For the very young child (fourth grade or below) the following explanation is effective: "The pair of eighths are partners because they are 'holding hands' (the eighth-note beam connecting the stems). They go through the beat together just as two children can hold hands and go through a doorway together." This is a far simpler, more direct, and more functional concept than "One-and" terminology builds.

The dotted-eighth-with-sixteenth grouping is called the "long short." In speaking, we dwell at length on the word "long," thus: "l-o-n-g short," completing both words before the beat runs out: "Notice that these two notes are still 'partners.' They are joined together by the beam across the stems, but now it is as if the teacher took hold of hands with one of the children and they went through the doorway together. The teacher fills up more space in the doorway than does the child, yet they still go through the door *at the same time.*"

As the classes progress, more difficult "partnerships" are encountered. For example, those in which one of the partners is a rest—a "silent partner" so to speak. In the chart the large type signifies speaking with emphasis. Part-NERS designates an eighth rest plus an eighth note, whereas PART-ners describes an eighth note coupled to an eighth rest. Again, the eye is trained to group the two symbols together into one unified beat.

Notice, too, the terminology for four sixteenth notes: "Four-on-one-beat." This is important. If the child should say, instead, "Four-on-a-beat" he will be speaking a triplet of sixteenths followed by an eighth.

In all of the terminology given, the thing that goes through the mind is exactly what has to come out of the hands in the performance. What the mind thinks the hands will perform.

When the student is ready to play such meters as $\frac{3}{8}$, $\frac{4}{8}$, $\frac{6}{8}$ in slow tempo, then we tell him that we are now going to call the eighth note "one." "Then how much will the quarter note get?" we ask him. His prompt answer is "Two beats." Thinking the eighth note as "one" it takes two sixteenths to make a partnership, and we go on from there.

Let us now extend the information of the chart into the fast $\frac{6}{8}$, $\frac{9}{8}$, and $\frac{12}{8}$ notation, where three eighth notes constitute one beat. Whereas in $\frac{0}{4}$

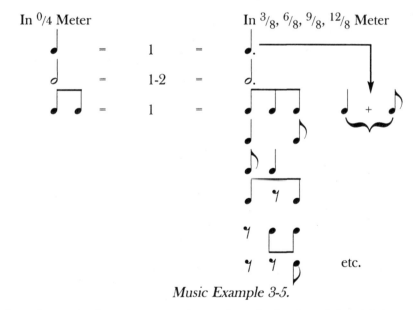

In $\frac{0}{4}$ Meter   In $\frac{3}{8}$, $\frac{6}{8}$, $\frac{9}{8}$, $\frac{12}{8}$ Meter

Music Example 3-5.

time signatures the quarter note is one beat, in the fast triplet-eighth meters, the quarter note is still the unit for one beat but *it now has a dot added to it.* In the $\frac{0}{4}$ signature, the half note is "one-two"; in the triplet-eighth meters, *the half note plus the dot* is "one-two." Thus we can make the comparisons given in Music Example 3-5. The three eighths of the triplet meter may be broken down into their equivalents as shown.

Quick recognition habits such as these, thoroughly acquired in the initial stages of learning, can smooth the path all the rest of the way, even into the professional field. Why don't we teach time-counting this way and make life really easy for the young musician? After all, this is the way we ourselves read as professionals. (After seeing a demonstration of this type of teaching, one violinist from a professional orchestra exclaimed excitedly, "But that is the *only* way you can read modern music!--by knowing what to do on each beat as it goes by.")

THE THREE CARDINAL SINS OF SIGHT-READING

Three special stumbling-blocks for the school orchestra player in sight-reading performances have emerged over the years. They are: (1) the half note, (2) the dotted-quarter with the eighth, and (3) a measure starting on an initial quarter note followed on the second beat by notes of lesser value (notes that have to be played faster than the quarter note because there are more of them per beat). Students are also confused by rests, especially when they are inserted frequently between the notes in a passage.

THE HALF NOTE

In practically every measuring system we use, zero is the starting point. But in time-counting we say "One" when the beat begins and then we have to wait for that beat to complete itself--to prolong itself into its "one" duration. For the children: "Suppose a man wants to get two pounds of sugar. He puts an *empty* bag on the scales and begins to pour in the sugar. In a few moments enough sugar has gone into the bag for the scales to register one pound. He continues to pour in more sugar, and soon the scales registers two pounds. But in music time-counting we say 'One' when the bag is empty—when the beat starts—so we have to wait for the beat to complete itself *after* we call it. In playing the half note, be sure to wait for that second beat to complete itself before you play the next note. Remember, when you say 'Two,' the beat is just starting. The next note (or rest) will come ON 'Three'." On the blackboard: One - - - - - Two - - - - - showing duration by the line following the numerals.

THE DOTTED-QUARTER-AND-EIGHTH

The too-early use of the "and" terminology in the dotted-quarter-and-eighth figure confuses youngsters. Children in the fourth grade have not yet had much to do with fractions and their minds do not work easily with them. (The "new mathematics" currently being taught is attempting to remedy this situation. Time alone will tell whether the ultimate results are better or worse than that which has gone before.) In the approach to time-counting that has been prevalent all these years, the teacher tells the child, "'One' is the beat and 'and' is the half beat." This seems to be quite clear until the youngster encounters

[2] The device of writing a quarter note and two eighth notes, then of tying the quarter to the first of the eighths is also excellent. One of the "partners" has joined a new corporation (the quarter note).

the dotted-quarter-and-eighth. Then he begins to have trouble. He starts on the dotted-quarter, and then plays the eighth too soon. The teacher begins to drill. "Johnny, how long should the dotted-quarter last?" Johnny answers correctly, "A beat and a half," and tries again to play the figure. Again the eighth comes too soon (actually, Johnny is playing it just before the second beat falls.) The teacher stops him: "But Johnny, you said the dotted quarter gets a beat and a half." For the third time, Johnny plays it incorrectly. If the teacher will ask Johnny just one more question, he will see where the trouble is. "Johnny, how do you count the dotted quarter?" Johnny replies benignly, "One-and." (!) After all, isn't this exactly what you told him in the beginning? "'One' is the beat and 'and' is the half beat."[2] The trouble was that what you (with your adult knowledge of fractions) were thinking was not at all what Johnny (without knowing fractions) was thinking at the time.

With the Unit Time-counting System, the problem can be quickly clarified: "Johnny, look here. A quarter note gets how much?" Johnny replies, "One beat." "All right. Now, the dot *lengthens* the note so it must get part of—?" "Two!" And suddenly Johnny smiles as light dawns. He is now secure and that rhythmic figure will not bother him further. The trouble was one of terminology, basically. The excess "and" after "One" served no useful purpose. (Just what Papa Mozart was talking about!) This figure, counted in the Unit System, would be stated clearly as "One—Two-and," which is what it *really* is. The thought that now passes through the mind is exactly what the music requires for its correct execution.

THE INITIAL QUARTER NOTE FOLLOWED BY NOTES OF LESSER VALUE

When a measure starts on a quarter note and shows faster notes (usually sixteenths) on the second beat, the students often precipitate the sixteenths, bringing them in ahead of the beginning of their proper beat. (Probably the mind alerts itself when the notes start getting "black" and the blood pressure rises to meet the exciting situation.) Emphasis here should be laid on the same fact that *"the quarter note fills up one whole beat."* No matter what a composer writes after the first quarter note in a measure (be it a sixteenth rest, a half note, a dotted quarter, or whatever), *"We must wait until 'Two' to start it."*

SPLITTING THE BEAT

To build complete fractional accuracy of execution, the common counting methods of "one-ti-tu-ti" and such other devices are excellent. But let us remember that these belong in the field of "higher musical mathematics," especially in stringed instrument instruction. Due to the complexity of the bi-manual problem, the mental approach to time-counting should be made as simple as humanly possible in its first stages.

In advanced work, thirty-second note relationships must be established. Using the quarter note as the unit for the beat, there are eight thirty-second notes per beat. Quick recognition of this grouping is very useful. However, when the music bristles with thirty-second notes, it is usually written in a slow tempo, so that the more practical approach is through making one eighth note equal one beat. Four thirty-second notes then make one beat. A sixteenth plus two thirty-seconds also equal one beat. And so on. These recognitions have to be instantaneous. There is no time, as the beats move steadily onward, to stop and figure them out.

In all of the foregoing methodology, the basic pedagogic principle has been: Whatever goes through the mind will come out of the hands. If the mind thinks too slowly, the hands begin to fumble. If the mind thinks inaccurately, the hands play the mistake. The quicker and more accurately the association centers of the brain function, the easier the reading process becomes; the quicker and more accurately the mind works, the finer the results in the whole technical equipment of the musician.

SOME APPLIED METHODOLOGY

When the time-counting has been learned by the Unit Method as recommended herein, the applications are tremendous. Let us observe that the continual reiteration of the customarily taught "One-two-three-four" terminology, in the counting of a number of measures of $^4/_4$ time, actually tells the *listener* nothing about the contents of those measures. It becomes merely a parrot-like repetition of a formula. Anyone can say "One-two-three-four" *ad infinitum* without thinking a thing. But the minute the youngsters use the terminology given in Music Example 3-2 (pages 38-39), their minds have to wake up and do some thinking. The association centers of the brain are immediately activated, for each symbol on the page presents the mind with "a problem to solve." The learning process steps ahead.

When children use the recommended terminology, anyone who is listening can tell, from what they say, exactly what is written on the page. (This is, obviously, impossible with the "One-two-three-four" method.) If a child misspeaks a symbol, the teacher knows immediately that there is a lack of understanding that needs attention.

As the children progress into the orchestra, the teacher can have several sections count their parts aloud (even simultaneously) using the Unit Method terminology. Incorrect wording on the part of any child will be immediately apparent. The teacher thus *knows* what each child is thinking. With the "One-two-three-four" system the child's mental processes are a deep, dark mystery. While the youngster may seem to be concerned with the notes, he may actually be engaged in a delightful fantasy about the Scout hike next Saturday. "One-two-three- - - -."

THE READING OF PITCHES

When the teacher wishes to stress the reading of pitches rather than of rhythm, the D-major scale is written on the chalkboard. (It may be notated in whole notes and in the several clefs in score form.) With a pointer the teacher guides the children through a chosen tune (such as "The First Nowell"), pointing it out note-by-note on the notated D scale. The pointer glides from one note to the next, never losing contact with the chalkboard and skillfully taking the eyes of the class with it. In this way new tunes may be introduced in unison. When a note is out of tune or incorrectly fingered by a child, the teacher can hold the whole class stationary on the particular note until the problem is solved. No one can move ahead of the class until the pointer shows what the next note is to be. We call this "Guided Reading." It is an excellent teaching device because the teacher is always in complete and flexible control of the situation.

Summing up this section. Once the eyes have seen the symbols (the notation) it is up to the mind to interpret, instantly and accurately, their meaning, both as to what pitch is to be played and how long it is to last. This has to be followed by correctly timed responses of the muscular structure in compliance with the mental directives. To strengthen this last factor, see the suggestions for practicing given on pages 76-77.[3]

READING THE CLEFS

Children find it interesting to read the clefs of the several stringed instruments. When the teacher wishes to interest some of the young violinists in changing to viola, it is fine to present the viola C-clef to the entire class. To introduce this clef, we first place the grand staff (treble and bass clefs) on the blackboard, with the middle-C note indicated on the leger line between the two clefs. By extending this middle-C line, and by adding to it the two lowest lines of the treble clef and the two top lines of the bass clef, we have the basic construction of the viola C-clef.[4]

[3]Ivan Galamian, *Principles Of Violin Playing And Teaching.* 2/E. 1985, pp. 15-17. Reprinted by permission of Prentice-Hall, Inc, Englewood Cliffs, New Jersey.

[4]Elizabeth A.H. Green, *The Modern Conductor,* 4/E, © 1987, pp. 138, 232. Reprinted by permission of Prentice-Hall, Inc., Englewood Cliffs, New Jersey.

Music Example 3-6 *

Attention should be called to the fact that the little pointer of the C-clef sign always designates middle-C on the staff.

When young violinists are playing viola clef on their violins and wish to produce the same sounds as the violists, they have only to move over one string lower, remembering that the open A (top string on the viola) is the second string on the violin.

This type of experience is especially valuable for the violin students because subtly they are accustoming their eyes to associate third position fingerings with the several lines and spaces of the staff. The fingerings in the viola clef are mechanically the same as the fingers used on the identical lines and spaces in the third position on the violin. (The sound, however, is different.) Music Example 3-7.

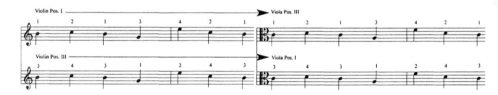

Music Example 3-7.

For the cellos, the top line of their bass clef is their open A; the space above it is the open A on the viola in the C-clef; so the cellists simply play each written note one step lower than notated. In this way they transpose the viola music down an octave and make it playable on their instruments, the cello being tuned exactly one octave lower than the viola. Contrast this clef sign with the position of the cellist's tenor C-clef on the staff.

Youngsters learn languages easily when they are young. They also take the clefs in stride if a natural and somewhat casual approach to them is made. Their attitude seems to be, "If Johnny can read that clef on *his* instrument, I can read it on mine, too."

THE SPELLING LESSON

Finally, to solidify knowledge of the fingerboard we can resort to the spelling lesson. Such words as bee, ebb, dab, cabbage, baggage can be "spelled" on the instrument, and the youngsters can be challenged to create great variety in the choice of fingering.

CHAPTER FOUR
LEFT HAND DEVELOPMENT

The left hand has three problems—intonation, shifting, and vibrato. As a vehicle for developing these techniques (as well as the many specialized uses of the bow) the scale is most useful. Scales can be fun on the stringed instruments and (adult opinion sometimes to the contrary) the children do not object to learning them when they form a basis for developing new techniques.

THE SCALES IN THE ORDER OF PRESENTATION

The one-octave scales can be presented in a sequence that will gradually develop the left hand from its original "natural" position (the half step between the second and third fingers) to its full extension (scales starting on second finger on violin and viola, and on first finger naturaled on cello).

The tendons of the ring finger join those of the middle finger in the lower part of the hand. For this reason, it is difficult at first to get much stretch between these two fingers. Thus, the most natural placement of the left-hand fingers is in a pattern that permits the second and third fingers either to work together as a unit (as they do on cello when the third finger plays F-sharp on the D string, both fingers coming down on the string at the same time), or permits them to touch each other as they rest upon the string (as in the playing of half steps on the violin and viola). Since the scale is comprised of two tetrachords of identical structure;

$$1 \quad 2 \quad 3 \underset{\vee}{\quad} 4$$
$$5 \quad 6 \quad 7 \underset{\vee}{\quad} 8$$

with the half step between the last two notes of each tetrachord, scales starting on an open string will have the same finger-pattern on two consecutive strings. This is true on violin, viola, and cello. The same is true for violin and viola when the scales start on the first finger. A one-octave scale starting on an open string on violin or viola places the half step between the second and third fingers on both strings thus using the easiest possible placement of the fingers. On the cello, the second and third fingers act as one unit (i.e., drop on the string at the same time) in the major scales starting on an open string; therefore, these scales are the easiest for that instrument, too.

The problem is more complicated on the string bass, since this instrument is tuned in fourths instead of fifths. Such tuning is necessary because of the size of the hand in relation to the size of the instrument itself. In bass fingering, the ring finger is not used for notes until the octave harmonic (half the length of the string) is reached. Therefore, this finger comes onto the string simultaneously with the fourth finger in the lower positions and there is no physical problem.

Whereas the violin, viola, and cello use stretches of the fingers to reach sharps and flats, the string bass substitutes the shifting of positions where necessary. Thus a scale starting on an open string on the bass will require a shift of position at its termination (Music Example 4-1). The last two notes are in half position while the rest of the scale is in first position.

The bass can be made to correlate with the other instruments in beginning instruction by using the notes of the D-major scale as given in

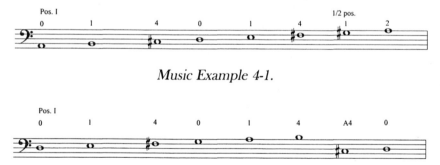

Music Example 4-1.

Music Example 4-2.

Music Example 4-2. (**Note:** This is a second version. See page 13 for the first version.)

Later on, the bass can slide into third position for the last C-sharp and D as shown in Music Example 4-3.

Music Example 4-3.

Attention should be called to the fact that the high D is on the G string, directly opposite the *curve* of the bass neck at the end where it joins the body of the instrument. This makes a good landmark for the youngster. Once in a while a bass is found that is not calibrated quite accurately, and the above statement will therefore not apply for that particular instrument.

Because of the variance in the fingering systems of the several stringed instruments, scales do not correlate easily as far as left hand difficulties are concerned. This is especially true if we try to eliminate the problem of shifting positions in the beginning stages of instruction.

Let us try to see what an ideal sequence for scale-proficiency might be on each of the four instruments individually, geared to the gradual muscular development of the left hand as it acquires skill on the individual instrument.

VIOLIN

Begin with the D-major scale and then apply the same fingering pattern to the scales starting on open A and open G. This gives us almost immediately three "open-string" scales: D-major, A-major, and G-major. Have the children play the three until they become easy.

Since these very first scales are usually taught without the use of the fourth finger, our next step is to get that finger into action by using scales that start on the first finger. These scales seem to be the most natural for the hand after its initial introduction to functioning on the instrument. They can be efficiently begun, by rote, about midway through the first semester's work. The first-finger scales, in order of presentation are: E-flat, B-flat, A-flat (starting on the G string); then E-major, B-major, and A-major (low octave starting on the G string).

To introduce these scales, we first have the children set the fingers on the D string, in correct position for the first four notes of the D scale: D, E, F-sharp, and G. We call attention to the fact that wherever there is an inch of vacant space there is also another note that can be played: "We are now going to finger these new notes. Let us first pull the second finger away from the third and fill in that space; then we shall pull the first finger back and fill in the space right next to the end of the string. This means that now first finger is at the end of the string, second finger is an inch away, and third finger is also an inch away. We shall now add the fourth finger, letting it rest right against the third finger, and we have our hand set for the new scale which uses all four fingers and all of the new notes."

Each note is plucked four times, the following finger being prepared for the next note during a fermata rest.

There seems to be less strain on the finger-muscles when the first, second, and third fingers are all spaced an inch apart than there is when first and second are touching each other on the string and the third finger alone has to make the inch stretch.

After the three flatted scales are learned, it is a simple matter to place the first finger a full inch from the end of the string (on the natural instead of the flat) and, using the same fingering sequence including the fourth finger, to produce the E-major, B-major, and (low octave) A-major scales. These first-finger scales introduce the use of the fourth finger in its easiest position, namely, resting on the string touching the third finger.

By presenting the first-finger scales at this time, with their accompanying flexibility of finger position on the string, rather than staying *ad infinitum* with the D-major scale pattern, we have laid a better foundation for rapid development and the subsequent skills of the left hand.

After the first-finger scales, we present scales starting on the *third* finger. (The scales that start on the second finger should come last. When they use the fourth finger instead of the open string they require the more difficult full extension of the hand-an inch between all fingers.) The two third-finger scales are G-major and C-major starting on the D and G strings respectively. In these scales the second finger touches the first finger, and the third finger acquires the independent muscular action mentioned previously.

Finally come the second-finger scales: F-major, B-flat major (starting on the G string), F-sharp major, and B-major. The student learns these scales using the fourth finger instead of the open strings, and thereby lays the foundation for the future three-octave scales with the Flesch pattern-fingering.[1]

VIOLA

The most logical order for scales on viola seems to be as follows:

> Starting on the open string: D scale, G scale, C scale.
>
> Starting on the first finger flatted: E-flat scale, A-flat scale, D-flat scale (beginning on the C string).
>
> Starting on the first finger natural: E-major scale, A-major scale, D-major scale (low octave), starting on the C string.

[1]Carl Flesch, *Scale System* (New York: Carl Fischer, Inc., 1926).

Starting on third finger: C scale, second octave; F-major scale.

Starting on the second finger: B-flat scale, E-flat scale, B-major scale, and the E-major scale.

Notice that in this procedure the foundation has also been laid for some two-octave scales since the student has acquired both the upper and lower octaves in several instances.

CELLO

For the cello scales we shall add, in parentheses, the string on which the first note of the scale is to be played.

Starting on the open strings: D scale, G scale, C scale.

Starting on fourth finger: C scale (second octave starting on the G string), F scale (C). Notice that these two scales start on the fourth finger which brings into play the review of the basic principle of starting out with all four fingers down on the string, thus insuring a good left-hand position.

Starting on the second finger: B-flat scale (G), which introduces the backward extension of the first finger. (See page 56 for the manner in which this extension is taught.) E-flat scale (C).

Starting on the first finger: A-major scale (G), which requires the forward extension of the second and fourth fingers; low-octave D-major scale (C).

Starting on the extended position of the second finger: B-major scale (G), and the E-major scale (C). (This is not a standard fingering for advanced cello playing.)

STRING BASS

The bass problem is more crucial since there are only three scales that can be played in a single position. These scales are:

In half position: B-flat scale starting with the first finger on the A string; F-major scale starting with the first finger on the E string.

In first position: G-major scale, starting with the second finger on the E string.

Scales requiring only one shift of position: A-major scale, starting on the open A string in first position and shifting to half position on the G string for the last two notes; E-major scale, starting on the open E string and shifting similarly on the D string.

Scales requiring two changes of position between half and first position: A-flat major, starting with the fourth finger in first position on the E string. The fingering is given in Music Example 4-4. (The accepted fingering for advanced playing starts 1, 4, in position 2 ½.)

Music Example 4-4.

Scales requiring more difficult shifts between the half and first positions: B-major, starting with the first finger on the A string; F-sharp major, starting with the first finger in first position on the E string and following the same sequence as the B-major scale, until the octave is reached. The B-major fingering is given in Music Example 4-5. The advanced fingering is added in parentheses below the notes.

Music Example 4-5.

CORRELATING ALL OF THE INSTRUMENTS

From the foregoing discussion it is easy to see that if the "ideal" order of presentation is followed for any one set of instruments, the others will automatically be handicapped all along the way in trying to correlate. Therefore, it is best to avoid pouring all of the students into the same mold in the presentation of the scales. Efficient individual progress can be made if the teacher will take a few minutes at the beginning of the class period to set up the finger pattern (plus its corresponding set of scales) for one family of instruments and, at the next class session, do the same for another group of players. In a few weeks the youngsters will have built some scale technique pertinent to their own instruments and thereafter certain correlations may be made. These, too, can follow a rather logical sequence so that no one section is constantly playing something too technically grueling. The correlating order might be as follows:

I. The beginning scale: D-major, starting on the open string for violins, violas, and cellos with the string bass using the accommodations shown in Music Examples 1-1, 4-2, and 4-3.

II. G scale, starting on the open string for violin, viola, and cello, and beginning with the second finger in first position on the E string in the basses.

III. A-major scale, starting on open A for the violins; the first finger on the G string for violas and cellos (the latter using the outward extension); open string, first position, for the bass, with the last two notes in half position.

IV. C-major scale, starting on third finger, G string, for violins and violas (the first and second fingers will touch); cellos, starting either on open C or on fourth finger on the G string. Basses, starting with the second finger, first position, on the A string and shifting to second position for the last note (fingering: 2 0 1 2 0 1 4-4). **Note:** The 4-4 fingering is not a good thing to do on bass, but we sometimes use it to locate clearly the exact position of the note for the child. The better scale fingering is to slide into second position after the note A on the G string (thumb drops about two inches down the back of the neck of the bass) and then to finger the last two notes 2-4.

V. F-major scale for violins and violas, with full extension of the hand; for cellos and basses, no problem.

VI. B-flat major scale. Violins with flatted first finger; violas starting with the second finger on the G string, full extension of the hand; cellos, backward extension of the first finger; basses, no problem.

VII. E-flat major scale. Violins and violas, backward extension of the first finger; cellos starting with the second finger on the C string, using the backward extension of the first finger on the next two strings. **Note:** Do not expect the cellos to start on the higher octave since this is one of the more difficult scales and marks the change in scale-shifting procedures. Basses, start with the first finger on the D string; after B-flat on the G string, drop to the fourth finger on the A string and continue upward from there.

VIII. E-major scale. Violins and violas, no problem. Cellos, starting with the first finger on the D string and using the long shift of that finger into fourth position for the last note of the scale. Still another and better fingering is as follows:

E	F-sharp	G-sharp	A	B	C-sharp	D-sharp	E
1	+2	+4	0	1	1 shift	3	4

Talented students may be challenged with this more difficult fingering. Basses, starting on open E, first position and going to half position on the D string.

PREPARING THE CELLO FINGER-EXTENSIONS

To prepare the cellist for the extension backward of the first finger, have him place all fingers on the D string in their normal, unextended position. Keeping the second, third, and fourth fingers on their notes, he lifts the first finger off the string and points it directly toward the ceiling (Fig. 4-1). He then leans it over until it contacts the string, not upsetting the other fingers. The point of contact of the first finger will be along the side of the finger-tip (Fig. 4-2). Set the first finger back again into its normal position and repeat this mechanic many times. When the first finger is actually sounding its flatted note, the other fingers should raise only slightly off the strings and should stay suspended over their notes while off the strings.

For the outward extension of the second and fourth fingers, the purpose of

Figure 4-1. Preparing the first-fingering extension on the cello.

Figure 4-2. Cello hand set in extension position.

which is to get the hand into such a position that it can play in tune on a fourth-finger sharped note, the first finger is "hooked" onto the string on its regular, naturaled note, and the second finger slides away from it to perform the note usually played by the third finger. This utilizes the stretch between the first and second fingers. As the second finger slides forward, the thumb also slides with it. The first finger, however, must remain on its note throughout. During the forward move of the thumb, the first finger gradually assumes the shape (and leans over onto the point of contact on the side of the fingertip) that it had when it made its own backward extension.

The extended position of the hand enables it to span the interval of the major third with relative ease and good intonation.

The Two-Octave Scale

There are several two-octave scales that can be used effectively on all four of the stringed instruments at one time. These are:

I. G-major scale: First position on violin, first octave starting on open G, second octave starting on third finger. First and third position on viola, shifting after second finger on the D string. First and fourth position on cello, shifting after the fourth finger on the A string. Positions I, III, V½ on bass, ending with the *third* finger on the octave harmonic on the G string. Fingering:

EA   D   G
2 0 1 2 0 1 4 0 1 4   shift 1 4   shift 1 4   3-harmonic

II. C-major scale: First position on viola and cello. First and third positions on violin, shifting after second finger on the A string; or, entirely in the third position. Bass: start with C on the A string, half position (fourth finger), then open D, and then drop to the low open E and proceed upward from there.

III. D-major scale: First position on viola and cello. First and third positions on violin, shifting after the second finger on the A string. Bass: start with open D and then drop immediately to the open E string and continue upward from there, first position, ending 2-4 in position III. (Music Example 4-3, page 51.)

IV. E-major scale: First position on viola, starting with the second finger on the C string. First and third positions on violin, shifting after the second finger on the E string and stretching the fourth finger for the high E harmonic. First and fourth positions on cello, shifting after the fourth finger on the A string. Slide on first finger to set up this important shift. String bass--start from open E.

As was mentioned before, the scales are excellent vehicles for building various skills in both hands. Once a scale has become easy for all of the students, the teacher can help them step ahead technically by superimposing various rhythms for the left hand and various types of bowing for the right hand.

INTONATION

The first step in good intonation is to get the instruments *in tune.* One recalls the *bon mot* of conductor George Dasch, "Almost in tune is still out of tune."

LEARNING TO TUNE THE INSTRUMENTS

Tuning is one of the more difficult aspects of beginning string playing. The first step is to learn the mechanics of handling the peg and making it stick. First the peg is turned *down,* pressing it into the instrument while turning. The peg works a little like a screw--it must be pushed into the instrument while being adjusted. This means that the hand holding the neck of the instrument must furnish a counter-pressure. It is the lack of counter-pressure that is at fault when the peg refuses to stay after the string has been tuned to pitch.

When the child cannot make the peg stick, the teacher can turn the peg while the child holds the neck of the instrument in one hand. By pushing hard on the peg, the teacher can force the youngster to give him a sufficient counter-pressure to make the peg stick. In this way the student acquires the feel of the amount of pressure needed.

BUILDING GOOD INTONATION

The sound of the piano intonation should be taught first if a piano is available. Frequent checking against the piano during the first year's study is strongly urged. Guard against pounding the keys and drowning out the youngster's sound. "Use the piano as a check, not a crutch."

The teacher may play either in unison with the students or at the octave. Chording can be added to the open string practice and as an accompaniment to the scales. In classrooms where there is no piano, the teacher will do well to bring his own major instrument (violin, cello, clarinet) and play counter-melodies to the class exercises. Intonation improves faster when the youngsters can hear note against note and when a solid standard is set by at least one player.

Students of the stringed instruments who do not hear the piano frequently enough in their first year of study often acquire a type of intonation that sounds rather convincing by itself but which is constantly under pitch when the piano enters the ensemble. After all, the standard of what **is** right should be built into the inner ear during the important first year of study. This is best done by use of the piano.

The second problem in building good intonation revolves around the refining of the half steps. On the violin especially the closeness of the fingers must be stressed if good half steps are to result. The fingers should touch each other on the strings. Certain intervals can be considered as being, technically, half steps on neighboring strings; the augmented fourth and the minor sixth.

Concomitantly with the drilling of the closeness of half steps comes the emphasis on the fully separated position of the fingers for whole steps—a "full inch of vacant space between the fingers." This too is largely a matter of acquiring the right concept for the sound. The imagination must be able to imagine the correct sound before the sound materializes from the instrument. Setting a correct hand position lays the foundation for easy realization of the imagined sound.

Notes that are constant trouble-makers are B-natural and F-natural. The former is usually under pitch (especially in double-stop playing), and the latter is usually too high. These two notes are the special province of the Junior High years and should be absolutely perfected during that time. The F-natural on the E string (violins) is especially given to being sharp. The finger is lazy in making its backward extension and before long the sharper, out-of-tune F begins to sound correct. Stress laid on the phrase "at the end of the string" will help.

In general, flats should have a lower, somewhat duller sound than their enharmonic equivalent in sharps. There is a distinguishable brilliance in the sound of a sharp; a softer, gentler sound in the flat.

Testing the third finger (violin and viola) or the fourth finger (cello) against the lower open string to check the octave intonation is excellent for the beginning student. On violin and viola the first and third fingers can always be

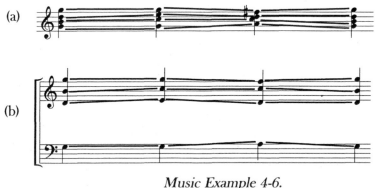

Music Example 4-6.

checked with the lower open string, the second and fourth fingers with the upper open string (first and third positions both). On cello the first and fourth fingers may be tested against the lower open string and the second and third fingers against the upper open string.

Professor Paul Rolland of the University of Illinois faculty recommends the following highly successful drill for youngsters in their first year of study. The sequence shown in Music Example 4-6 is placed on the blackboard.[2] Each child is assigned one series of notes, reading horizontally. In a homogeneous class the closed harmonic position is used (letter a); in the heterogeneous class, the open position functions (letter b).

The children quickly memorize the four simple patterns of note-sequence so that each child can play any of the four. The first chord of any given key is set up and then the youngsters proceed through the chordal sequence in harmony. This is an excellent device for teaching good intonation early in the learning process.

[2]Used by permission.

CHAPTER FIVE
ORCHESTRAL PLAYING
IN ITS EARLIER STAGES

T he entrance into the orchestra is a greatly anticipated event. Excitement climbs almost as high as it did that day a year ago when the youngsters took their instruments out of the cases and held them in their hands for the first time.

THE FIRST DAY IN ORCHESTRA

Let us now look in on that first rehearsal. The orchestra is seated and tuned. The conductor gives the initial instructions concerning the mechanics of the rehearsal; where to leave the cases, the importance of being there on time, the tuning procedures for the strings and winds, and the handling of the music itself. He should then take time to explain the important rehearsal routines; how the orchestra stays together, how important it is to stop instantly when the conductor's baton cuts off the music, how all must listen to each bit of instruction when the conductor stops the orchestra to "make repairs" — for he will stop only when something needs fixing.

The orchestra stays together by seeing and recognizing the down-beat in every measure. The first note of each measure is played on the conductor's down-beat. The conductor should explain: "If the notes are too hard in some measure and you miss them, don't give up and just sit there. Take a quick look at the first note in the next measure, then look at the baton and play that note on the next down-beat. This way you will be right back on the job and no one will ever know that you missed a couple of notes along the way. It is no sin to miss a note at this level of advancement, but it is a sin not to be able to get going again."

The first drill in reading the down-beat is to lay aside the music and have the youngsters simply observe the stick as the conductor beats an exercise such as this: $\frac{4}{4}$, $\frac{3}{4}$, $\frac{4}{4}$, $\frac{6}{4}$, $\frac{2}{4}$, $\frac{3}{4}$, $\frac{4}{4}$, $\frac{4}{4}$, $\frac{1}{4}$, $\frac{1}{4}$, $\frac{6}{4}$, $\frac{7}{4}$, $\frac{2}{4}$, $\frac{8}{4}$. The children count out loud, saying "One" whenever the stick makes the recognizable first-beat-of-the-measure and continuing to count until the next "One" appears thus: "*One*-two-three-four, *One*-two-three, *One*-two-three-four," and so on.

For the second drill, the conductor takes a tune from the music and, while beating all of the beats in each measure, has the orchestra play only the first note in each bar, matching it to the down-beat. If he wishes to make the problem harder, as skill matures, he can slightly vary the tempo from measure to measure.

(And now, Mr. Conductor! Take a look at your down-beat and make sure that it is so clear that a professional man would be well content with it. If your rebound after "One" is too high, no one can tell what you are doing. *The rebound of the down-beat should not go higher than half the height of the down-beat itself if real clarity is to eventuate.*[1] When the rebound of "one" climbs all the way back to the top, it makes the second beat (and often those that follow) look just like the first beat and the time-beating pattern becomes unreadable (Fig. 5-1).

On the first day in orchestra it is also good to have each section play a few measures alone so that the new players in the section can hear the sound they should distinguish as their own.

The melody line should be clarified by having it played in ensemble by those instruments that carry it in the various parts of the piece. Emphasize the fact that the melody *must* be heard, on any level of performance. The players with the melody line are "carrying the ball" at the moment and "the ball must get through."

Some drill in loud and soft playing, especially the latter, is excellent, so that eventually the conductor can get contrast into the various sections of the music.

STOPPING THE MUSIC

It is necessary, in the beginning, to show the children what a cut-off looks like so that they will stop when the conductor wishes to speak to them. Making the cut-off gesture and then dropping the baton completely out of sight is fine on the grade-school level. "If you can't see the stick, don't play." Continuing to wave the stick nervously around in the air with spasmodic gestures is not effective in producing silence.

Drill the youngsters in the habit of lifting the bow straight up and of taking the horn immediately away from the lips when the cut-off gesture is made. Such early training in alertness for these stops is not only a "fun" technique, but it

[1]Elizabeth A.H. Green, *The Modern Conductor*, 4/E, © 1987, pp 138, 232. Reprinted by permission of Prentice-Hall, Inc., Englewod Cliffs, New Jersey.

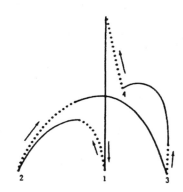
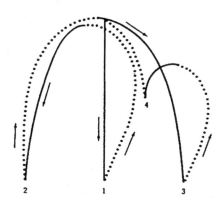

Readable beat.   Unreadable beat.
Dotted line shows the rebound.   Rebound goes back to top of down beat.

Figure 5-1.

will literally save hours of rehearsal time before those youngsters graduate from high school.

LEARNING TO BEAT TIME

Once the orchestra is well under way for the year, it is a good idea to teach the children to beat $\frac{3}{4}$ and $\frac{4}{4}$ time. (The $\frac{3}{4}$ pattern is the easiest.) In every group there are a few confident extroverts. Choose one of these for the first experience. Have him take the conductor's place on the podium and beat time for the orchestra. (Be sure to call it "beat the time" at this stage. Do not dignify it with the word "conduct.") While the first youngster is occupying the podium, the conductor can have a second youngster stand on the floor behind, rehearsing so that when the first one steps down the second one will be ready to take over. If each child has this chance to rehearse before he takes the podium, it will be possible eventually to get every child up front, even the timid ones.

There are two benefits that accrue. The first one is

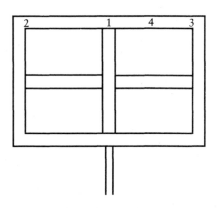

Figure 5-2. Diagram of music stand marked for time-beating.

that the rhythm of the entire group seems to solidify, sometimes in quite an amazing way. The second benefit is that the teacher now has some assistants who can lead the group for a few minutes at a time when he himself wishes to circulate among the players giving special help where needed.

The children should be taught the standard time-beating patterns, but without the use of the baton at first. If the four-beat pattern is troublesome-sometimes the youngster swings his down-beat all the way to the left because he is already thinking "left on Two" — the teacher can mark the top of the conductor's music stand as shown in Figure 5-2. The student then taps the stand as the numbers indicate.

Hearing the Individual Within the Group

The conductor often wishes to know what progress the individual player is making in the orchestra. There are two things that can help. The first is the "echo" solo. Let us say that the music reads as shown in Music Example 5-1. The orchestra plays the first two measures in the passage and then a pre-designated "soloist" performs all alone the next two measures, the orchestra tutti entering again after the solo. Children love to do this. It is a fine pre-training for that big solo later on in high school, and it gives the conductor a chance to hear the individual now and then.

Music Example 5-1.

The second thing that can be done is to choose a small ensemble (such as one flute, one violin, one cornet; or one violin, one clarinet, one trombone, and a muffled drum) and have the group take over for one strain somewhere in the piece. This too is fun for the players and most interesting for the audience. These soloists stand up when they play their solo passages. The orchestra is silent. A whole section may play its melody in the same manner, standing, and with soft orchestra accompaniment if desired.

How much Routining?

In addition to the reading of the down-beats, the attention to orchestral balance and the listening for the melody line, plus the various mechanical aspects of the running of the orchestra, the children should also be taught the following things: If music folders are used, they should learn to close them properly at the end of each rehearsal without folding the music up, one piece inside of another. "The folder must always be present at the rehearsal even if the player is not."

The string players should be introduced to the most elementary of the bow-direction principles used by the professional orchestra. (After all, the professional man knows how easiest to get his effects.) The first few bowing rules are simple and well within the grasp of the elementary school child:

1. Measures, in general, start down-bow and the down-bow matches the conductor's down-beat.

2. A single note before the bar line (preceded by a rest or coming at the beginning of a piece and not slurred) is taken up-bow.

3. An odd number of bows before the bar line (after a rest) should start up-bow.

4. An even number of notes (bows) before a bar line (after a rest) are started down-bow.

5. The slur over the bar line is down-bow.

6. In waltzes, the rhythmic figure "rest, quarter, quarter" is played down-bow, up-bow. The bow lifts off the string on each rest.[2]

The children should also understand that a "first chair" is not all glory, that it includes certain responsibilities, and that a good section leader must be a dependable person in fulfilling his duties. One of them is to set the bowing for the section.

HOW MUCH THEORY?

All youngsters, before they get out of grade school, should understand the basic structure of the major scale with its half steps and whole steps. The strings especially should be able to start on any pitch and build thereon a major scale, applying their knowledge and using their ears.

Note: The ability to think scalewise is far too neglected in much of our school work. When college-age students sing fifths for major seconds, and sing thirds for fifths, there is something wrong with the way they have been taught. *The mind should be able to fill in, scalewise, all missing notes between the terminal ends of any interval.* If it can do this, the final note of the interval will emerge on correct pitch. This building of the "inner" hearing ability should be strengthened first by hearing and playing many scales.

The youngsters should know about the transposing instruments, that the

[2]E. A. H. Green, *Orchestral Bowings and Routines.* (Ann Arbor, Mich.: Campus Publishers, 1949, 1957), pp. 81-82. Used by permission.

cornet and clarinet sound one whole tone lower than the flutes and strings when they are playing the same printed notes.

All should understand the principle of the grouping of notes so that their total always equals one beat. For good sight-reading one must *know how much of the music to play on each beat and then do it.*

It is also fine if the strings have been alerted to the existence of the three clefs, G-clef, F-clef, and C-clef, and feel well enough acquainted with them that they will not approach them with fear in their advanced work. After all, these are perfectly normal adjuncts of the orchestral world.

CHAPTER SIX
SUBSEQUENT BOWING
DEVELOPMENT

Throughout the student's training the bowing skills should receive constant attention. Whereas the left-hand fingers set the pitches, it is the bow that actually makes them sound. During the second year of study (1) good progress should be made in the breadth and quality of the détaché stroke, (2) the martelé (the press-release-play bowing) should be begun on the violin and viola and continued on the lower instruments, (3) attention should be given to the sustaining of the full bow stroke without fluctuation and with a good quality of tone, and (4) the spiccato can be started.

The first part of the second year can be given over to the Eight Fundamental Bowings during which time a noticeable growth in skill and particularly in sound will take place.

THE EIGHT FUNDAMENTAL BOWINGS

The Eight Fundamental Bowings are so called because they form a detailed development of the whole-bow stroke and lay the foundation for the two basic types of accommodation which the bow has to make. The accommodations are: (1) the allotting of an equal amount of bow to each note played–the speed, pressure, and distance from the bridge remaining a constant throughout, and (2) the variation of speed of stroke to accommodate a varying number of beats per bow. In this latter case, the problem is to keep the dynamic steady as the bow changes its speed. When such a change occurs, both the distance from the bridge and the pressure factor have to be given special attention. Figure 6-1 (p.69) presents these bowings.

The first six of the eight bowings deal with the equal allotment of bow to each note played. This means that the bow moves steadily across one place in the string without changing its distance from the bridge and with a constant, unwavering pressure and unchanging speed of stroke. This should result in an even dynamic on each note.

The last two of the bowings concern themselves with the variation in speed of the bow's motion. To play bowings 7 and 8, one stroke has to move three times as slowly as the other. This requires the slower stroke to play a little closer to the bridge with a slightly heavier pressure, while the faster stroke moves farther from the bridge and releases some of the pressure.

The first three bowings use exactly half of the bow for each note played. In the first two, the section of the bow indicated should be perfected, using the entire half of the bow and keeping it ideally straight. Bowing number 3 combines 1 and 2 into a single exercise, the purpose of which is to prepare for bowing number 4, the full-bow stroke. Bowing number 4 smooths out the motions of bowing number 3 resulting in the fine, long, frog-to-point use of the entire length of the bow. In 5 and 6, the slur should find the finger changing as the middle of the bow is passed. These two bowings are obviously a combination of the techniques built up in bowings 4, 1, and 2.

On violin and viola, bowing number 7 should add to the fast down-bow the forward fling of the arm just as the point of the bow is approached. If this forward motion does not occur on a fast down stroke, the tip of the bow will be seen to slide away from the bridge. On the slower up-bow, the bow-arm will retract rather quickly its forward position.

In bowing number 8, on all instruments, the fast up-bow comes off the string (as a practice routine) just after the middle of the bow has been passed, and the bow is set immediately at the frog again for the next down stroke which follows without pause. This lifting may have to be exaggerated at first with the younger student. It should not be a skimming for the string, but should cleanly come off from the string. Its purpose is to train lightness into the stroke as the frog is approached on a fast up-bow. Later on the bow can remain close to the string when it is lifted off.

On violin and viola, the tipping of the bow toward the scroll, just before the lift, will ease the feeling in the arm and hand as the bow comes off the string. Exaggerating the height of the lift the very first few times, using a dotted half note (down-bow) and a quarter note (up-bow) on an open string will also help the feeling of free play in the bow arm. Using the outer edge of the hair on violin and viola when the bow is set at the frog helps to prevent scratchiness in the tone which is due to too much pressure on the string at this heavy end of the bow.

1. △ to □ ○ (frog to middle)

Each written note is played four times. Bow on the outer edge of the hair at the frog.† Go way to the frog on each up-bow. Guard against shrugging the shoulder when practicing this bowing.

2. □ to point (middle to point)

The bow arm moves forward gradually on the down-bow and gradually backwards on the up-bow. This motion should be perfected during the practice of this bowing. The straightness of the bow should be ideally perfect at the tip. (Violin and viola.)

3.

THINK! 1. "Stop at the square (middle)," then play the first note and stop. 2. "Forward to the point," then play the second note and see that the arm moves forward as well as outward, and stop. 3. "Backward to the middle," and see that the arm retracts its forward stretch so that the bow is perfectly straight at the middle, and stop. 4. "On the edge to the frog," and stop. The thought must precede the action during this important third bowing.

4. One whole bow per written note.

Move from the very frog all the way to the point. Each note is played only one time from here on. The motions developed individually in bowing 3 are now smoothed out into one uninterrupted stroke. (Violin and viola.)

5.

Use the whole bow (bowing 4) on the slur, then the half bow (bowing 2) on the next two notes, bowing 4 on the next slur and bowing 1 on the last two unslurred notes of the measure.

6.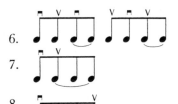

The reversal of 5. Bowing 1, 4, 2, 4.

7.

Fling forward on the down-bow and recover backward on the up-bow.

8.

Lift after each up-bow and reset the bow at the frog for the next down stroke. All four instruments.

○ The "triangle" is formed by the shoulder to elbow to point of contact of bow on string, when the bow is at the frog. The "square" forms in the approximate middle of the bow, with some variation for individual arms. (Violin and Viola.)
† Inner edge, Cello and Bass.

Figure 6-1. The eight fundamental bowings.

Perfecting one of the eight bowings each week, taking them in the prescribed order (this can be done either in the orchestra[1] or in the class lesson), and using the same etude throughout, should produce a fine step ahead in bow control and in sound by the time all eight have been conquered. (In private lessons these bowings are usually done in pairs, two per week.) Children have been heard to remark, "It's fun to practice this way."

Ideal straightness of the bow-stroke should be *perfected* during this period. The mirror can be of great help in getting an objective view of the bow and its relationship to the string. Keeping the bow straight in the mirror, the arm gradually acquires the *feel* of the straight bow-stroke. One must stand with the violin parallel to the mirror and the **right shoulder toward the mirror.**

To progress rapidly the mind must be alert during practice. It cannot go off "wool-gathering" while the hands perform mechanically. To alert the mind, give it problems to solve, problems which will require it to think. The Eight Fundamental Bowings provide problems for the youngster at this level of advancement.

Bowings 5, 6, 7, and 8 will increase the synchronization of the two hands. Refer to the suggestions for advanced practice, page 76, in this book.

DÉTACHÉ, MARTELÉ, AND SPICCATO

The détaché should show noticeable improvement in sound and freedom of stroke after the eight fundamental bowings are conquered. Basically, this stroke is a broad, un-slurred rendition of each note, smoothly connected. The word *détaché* means detached only in the sense of "not slurred." It does not mean detached in the sense of staccato, or spacing between notes. The smoothness and continuousness of the sound as the bow changes direction is part of the skill of the détaché. Flexibility of wrist and fingers is important in this bowing.

The martelé is the staccato stroke. While the bow is standing still it depresses the string by pressing on it; then, when the bow starts to move, most of the pressure is released instantaneously. If this bowing starts to move with full pressure applied to the string, an unpleasant roughness will result. When the stroke is mastered, it will sound a clean-cut articulation similar to sharp tonguing on a wind instrument. The martelé should be practiced slowly for there is a definite limit to the speed at which it can be performed due to the stopping and setting of the bow-pressure before each stroke. Youngsters often describe this bowing as "the one where you take more time to get ready than you do to actually play it."

[1]Wohlfahrt, Op.45, Book I, number 1, can be found for full orchestra in unison in Volume I, *Musicianship and Repertoire,* by Green, published by Theodore Presser Company, Bryn Mawr, Pennsylvania, 1962.

The control of the pressure factor comes from a leverage between the stick of the bow and the fingers. On violin and viola, this leverage starts with the upward thrust of the curved thumb and the opposite pressure of the first finger on the stick of the bow. The bow-hand also leans into the stick which forces the wrist to turn slightly and to add its pressure to that of the first finger. On cello and bass, the leverage comes from a somewhat less-curved thumb pushing forward, and the first finger resisting that forward push by pressing inward, toward the string. Here also the wrist responds to the pressure.

The spiccato is a stroke in which the bow is dropped onto the string and rebounds off the string, straight up, after every note. One approach to this bowing, which has proved effective in helping to gain skill, is to isolate the resiliency factor first. The bow is actively flung down on the string and allowed to rebound, the hand and arm making no down-bow, up-bow motion whatsoever. After the bow hits the string, it reacts against the first finger of the bow hand, forcing the hand to turn as if pivoting around an axis. The motion in the violin and viola bow-hand is similar to the turning of a door knob. In this first step, little if any tone sounds. The bounding of the bow, on and off the string, is all that occurs. The section of the bow used is just a little closer to the frog than the exact middle of the bow. After the isolation of the bounce becomes extremely easy and is continuous, add the second step: the down-bow, up-bow stroke in the same rhythm. At this stage the tone will be very rough, for the important thing is to continue the freedom of the bounce. The bow will hit two strings. The third step is to drop the bow more gently so that it does not fly off the string quite so far. It will be found that the A string (or D string) alone emerges and the tone loses its roughness. The final step is applicable only to violins and violas, and this step is to tilt the stick of the bow slightly toward the pegs of the violin so that the hair contacts the string a bit on its outer edge. The tone will then begin to ring with resonance. The hand holds the bow lightly for this stroke.

Each of these steps should be perfected before the next one is attempted. Begin with the mechanical bounce and stay with it until the hand and arm relax and permit the bow to carry on. When this step has become easy add the down-bow, up-bow motion, and then the gentle bounce. Usually a student can spend a week on each step.

The material in this chapter deals with the problems of the bow during the second and third years of work. However, much of it can also be used to good advantage in the junior and senior high school orchestras to perfect further an already usable technique.

CHAPTER SEVEN
INCREASING THE PROFICIENCY

The following discussion deals with the several facets of stringed instrument playing that are common to all four of the stringed instruments.

WRIST FLEXIBILITY IN THE BOW HAND

VIOLIN-VIOLA

There is no better exercise for building wrist flexibility than a constant crossing between the same pair of strings (Music Example 7-1).

In Music Example 7-1 the lower string is played down-bow and the upper string up-bow. On the down-bow the stick is tipped toward the bridge and on the up-bow away from the bridge toward the scroll. *Only the section of the bow between the middle and the point should be used for this exercise.* The tipping of the bow from edge to edge should be done by the whole hand moving in the wrist joint, not by twisting the stick between the fingers.

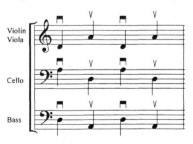

Music Example 7-1.

CELLO-BASS

Here the direction of the bow-stroke is just the reverse. The upper note is played down-bow and the lower note up-bow. Throughout both strokes the bow plays on the inner edge of the hair, stick toward ceiling. The wrist will precede the hand in the drawing of the down-bow thus assuming a flatter position. On the up-bow the hand will drop downward from the wrist thus performing the crossing to the lower pitched string. Any section of the bow may be used on these instruments.

SLURRING ACROSS STRINGS

In slurring across strings the left-hand fingers should remain in position on both strings until the bow has safely established itself on the new string. The bow's motion is in the form of a slow arc, performed with great smoothness. Letting the doublestop sound momentarily, in slow practice, is a fine device. Slight pressure may be added to the bow as it nears the new string after the initial slow stages of control have been completed.

DYNAMICS

The louder tones are played with the bow nearer the bridge, and using slightly more pressure and moving at a slower rate of speed. The softer tones may be either close to the fingerboard with the bow moving very lightly and a bit faster, or slightly nearer the middle of the playing range with a much slower stroke. Pressure and speed always have to balance each other for the distance from the bridge.

LONG SUSTAINED TONES

When a long tone must be sustained forte, the bow should travel toward the bridge as the point is approached, adding slightly more pressure and moving slowly.

DOUBLE-STOPS

The problem in double-stop performance is a bowing one: To get the two notes started together and then to keep them both sounding throughout the stroke. For this reason it is best to have the first-encountered double-stops bowed many times, not just once. Take a simple set of double stops and bow each pair a dozen times before changing to the next double-stop. Fig. 7-1 shows the bowing planes for the A and E strings on the violin. The bow in the center bisects the angle made by these two bow levels. Such a placement of the bow enables it to contact evenly both strings. when children play with a poor quality of tone on double stops, it is usually because the angle of the bow is not

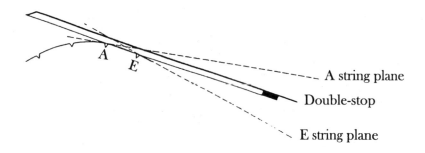

A string plane

Double-stop

E string plane

Figure 7-1. Diagram depicting bow angles for double-stop playing.

correct and one string is getting more pressure from the bow than is the other string.

PIZZICATOS

There are some tricks here. Speaking of the string bass, the softest pizzicatos are plucked mid-way between the bridge and the finger holding down the note to be sounded. The next loudest place to pluck is at the bridge end of the fingerboard, and the loudest is *right next to the fingered note.* For very high notes on the violin, played pizzicato, there is customarily little if any resonance. But it is possible, by varying the place where the string is plucked, to find an individual resonance-peak for every note.

THE VIBRATO

VIOLIN-VIOLA

The third position seems to be the easiest place for setting the hand to begin the vibrato motion. Place the lower edge of the palm against the lower edge of the body of the violin, the hand resting in the third position. Make a hinge of this point of contact and let the hand rock back and forth (Fig. 7-2). Next, place the second finger on the string very lightly and let it slide down and up the string as the rocking motion continues. The motion must be rhythmic and it must be interspersed with frequent rests. When the rocking-sliding motions have become really easy and very rhythmic, make less motion until the finger comes to rest on one note (E on the A string is good). The hand continues to rock and the second finger, sitting on its note, becomes a sort of pivot or fulcrum for the motion. Of utmost importance is the fact that the side of the first finger must be free of the instrument. In the setting of the hand, there must be no sidewise curve in the wrist. The hand must be set well to the right side of

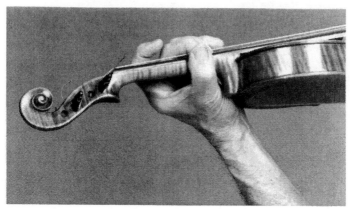

Figure 7-2. Violin hand set in vibrato position.

the neck of the instrument so that there is a straight line from the elbow to the base of the middle finger (Fig. 7-2).

After the vibrato is perfected with each finger in the third position, it will transfer easily to the first position provided the arm is brought around enough to the right to permit the side of the first finger to cease to contact the neck of the instrument.

Cello-Bass

The hand is set in the fourth position. The motion comes from the elbow and the entire lower arm moves as a unit. Start with the sliding of the second finger up and down the string (just as in the violin vibrato). On the cello, the side of the hand can rhythmically impinge on the upper rib of the body of the instrument. When this sliding motion is easy, set the finger solidly on a note and continue the up-down motion of the arm. One caution: the entire lower arm should feel the down-up motion, and it should not be confused with a rolling motion pivoting around a lengthwise axis. The latter does not produce the best vibrato for these instruments.

Practicing for Proficiency

The practice story can be condensed into three simple approaches for the intermediate student. These apply to all four of the stringed instruments.

(1) If separately-bowed notes are bad, especially where many string-crossings occur, practice the passage diligently with a martelé bowing. This will help to clean up the attack of each note even if the final rendition of the passage is détaché.

(2) If the left-hand fingers tangle or stumble, the passage should first be played half a dozen times *very slowly* to give the ear a chance to hear what the

[1]Ivan Galamian, *Principles Of Violin Playing And Teaching*, 2/E, © 1985, pp. 15-17. Reprinted by permission of Prentice-Hall, Inc., Englewood Cliffs, New Jersey.

passage really sounds like. Then the following basic rhythms may be superimposed[1] (Music Example 7-2). Practicing with various rhythms sets up problems for the left hand to solve and when the student has *conquered* the passage with several different rhythms, he will find that he has built more technique on the passage than is needed in order to play it easily in its original form.

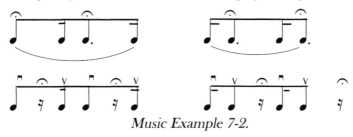

Music Example 7-2.

(3) If bow and fingers do not synchronize, mix slurs with separately bowed notes in a definite pattern. In this way one sets up problems for the bow to solve. Conquer the passage with several of the new bowings and the synchronization of the two hands will gradually improve. The last four of the Eight Fundamental Bowings (Fig. 6-1) are pertinent here.

One final word of caution. In all of the foregoing practice methods, and in the use of the various types of bowings discussed in the preceding chapter, the teacher must be sure that the child is ready for them. They are not elementary problems. The practice methods should be delayed until the student has arrived at the point of proficiency where he can *apply* the techniques called for. In other words, his attention should be centered on the *music* he is learning and on the application of the routines to it rather than on the basic learning of the routines themselves.

THE POSITIONS

There are seven basic positions. These are numbered on all four instruments by the succession of letter-names-of-notes going up the A string. First finger on B is first position; first finger on C is second position; first finger on D, third position, and so on. The bass has also half positions, occurring between the regular position on the half steps. Fig. 7-3 shows the correlation of the positions on all four stringed instruments.

SHIFTING POSITIONS

Smoothness and accuracy are the goals in shifting from one position to another. On the violin the shifts between the four lowest positions are performed by bending the elbow thus drawing the hand farther up the instrument

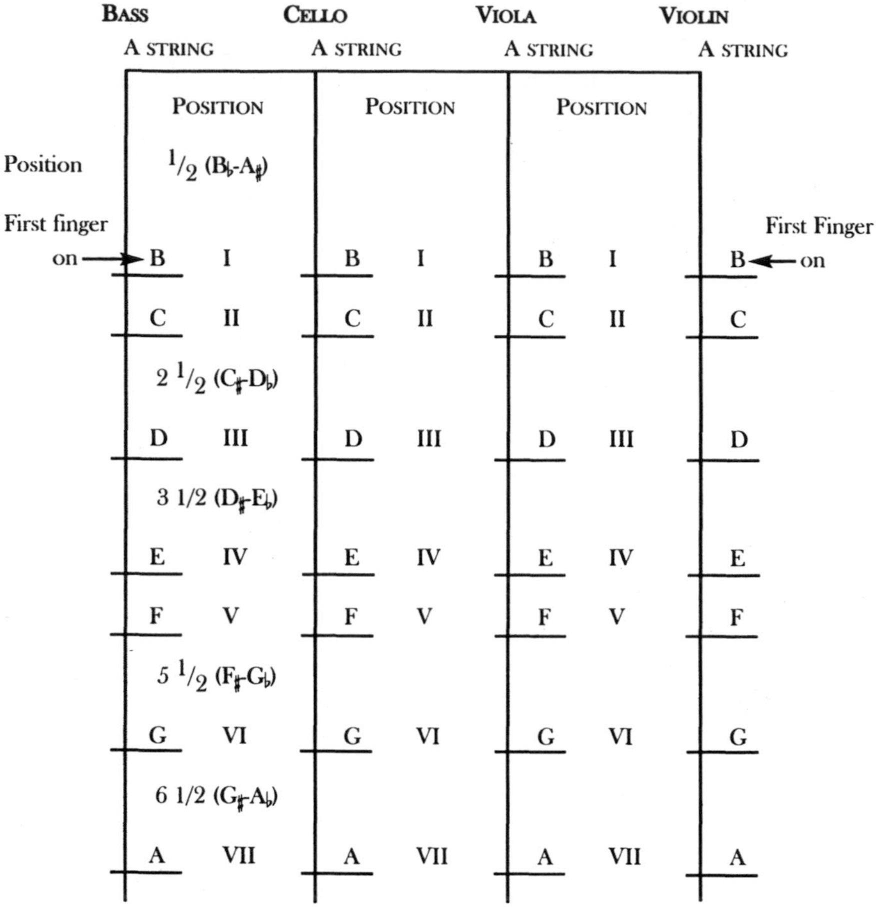

BASS		CELLO		VIOLA		VIOLIN	
A STRING		A STRING		A STRING		A STRING	
POSITION		POSITION		POSITION			
Position	$^1/_2$ (B♭-A♯)						
First finger on →	B I	B I	B I	B ← on
	C II	C II	C II	C
	$2\,^1/_2$ (C♯-D♭)						
	D III	D III	D III	D
	3 1/2 (D♯-E♭)						
	E IV	E IV	E IV	E
	F V	F V	F V	F
	$5\,^1/_2$ (F♯-G♭)						
	G VI	G VI	G VI	G
	6 1/2 (G♯-A♭)						
	A VII	A VII	A VII	A

First Finger on (at right of VIOLIN column, level with B)

Figure 7-3. Chart showing the correlation of the seven positions on all four of the stringed instruments.

or pushing it back toward first position. On the cello the shift of position is accomplished by dropping the hand down the fingerboard or raising it again through action in the elbow joint. On the bass the thumb drops approximately two inches down the neck for each half-position (half step) shifted.

GENERAL PRINCIPLES OF SHIFTING

(1) The finger that is on the string when the shift starts completes the slide into the new position and the finger required in the new position comes straight down onto its note. (2) **Exception:** When a shift to a higher numbered position goes to a finger of lower number than the finger that is on the string when the

shift starts, the lower numbered finger takes over during the shift and completes the slide into the new position. This is to prevent over-sliding the required pitch. (3) In slurred shifts the bow should slow down its motion just before the finger starts its slide to the new position. If this is not done, a bad smearing sound results since the use of much bow during a shift highlights the slide. Generally speaking, the finger making the slide can lighten its pressure during the slide, but it must not lose contact with the string entirely. The note before the shift should be played strongly and with sufficient length to "cover" the sound of the following slide. The note on which the slide terminates must be given attention for good intonation.

Caution the student to remember that a shift of position means a new position for the *thumb*. Stretching the fingers from one position to another with the thumb remaining static is NOT a change of position.

On the violin and viola, the odd-numbered fingers (1 and 3) play all notes on lines in the odd-numbered positions (I, III, V, VII, etc.). The even-numbered fingers play the lines in the even-numbered positions. Fifth position fingers the same as first position but with the fingers placed one string lower.

On the cello, fourth position fingers like first with the same fingers playing the notes that are an octave higher than the first position notes (Music Example 7-3).

Music Example 7-3.

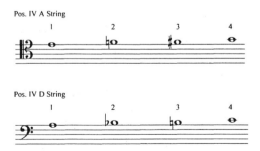

Music Example 7-4.

Tenor clef fingers like bass clef but the fingers are placed one string higher (Music Example 7-4).

On the bass, the half positions finger as if every note of the preceding position were sharped or every note of the following position were flatted, i.e., raised or lowered a half tone.

The thumb position on cello and bass starts with the octave of the open string (seventh position) and the fingering becomes similar to that of the violin, each finger playing its own sharps and flats. Third finger is substituted for fourth on the bass in the thumb position since the fourth finger can no longer reach the strings.

For the positions I through IV, cello and bass, the thumb and second finger remain opposite each other as the hand slides up and down the neck of the instrument.

Chapter Eight
String Vibration, Sympathetic Vibration, and Harmonics

A vibrating string is fascinating to watch. Pluck a string and notice how it twists and turns after the plucking finger has completed its action. The string seems almost to come alive. In bowed tone-formation, the bow has "to take the string with it" as it moves from frog to tip and back. Watching the string to see if its vibration pattern is steady and not interrupted throughout the whole length of the bow-stroke is a fine exercise.

Sympathetic Vibration

There is a "law of nature" that is most important to the player of the stringed instrument. It is called the law of sympathetic vibration and is as follows: Given: two objects tuned exactly to the same pitch. One of them is set into vibration, thus sending sound waves out into the air. When these waves impinge upon the second object it, too, will begin to vibrate of its own accord.

This principle is tremendously important in both intonation and resonance in the stringed instrument. In application it means simply this: If one were to play a second-space treble-clef A, up on the G string of a violin, and if this A were played exactly in tune with the open A, the latter would immediately begin to vibrate, too. Figure 8-1 shows this phenomenon. In this picture, the bow is contacting only the G string. Notice that the A string is vibrating freely in sympathy with the A on the G string, but that the D string is standing perfectly still showing that there is no contact of the bow with that string.

When the A string adds itself to the tone of the A on the G string, it produces a fine resonance and a lustre in the sound that cannot be achieved in any other way. Not only will open strings respond in this way but their natural

Figure 8-1. Sympathetic vibration of the A string on the violin.

harmonics will also respond. A string will break itself up into nodal sections (more of this in a moment) in sympathy with other perfectly-tuned tones on the instrument.

PRODUCING AUDIBLE HARMONICS

Every time a string player depresses the string solidly down to the finger-board a new pitch, called a fundamental, materializes. He can produce many more fundamentals than our musical system calls for, because each time he plays "out of tune" he has a new fundamental. One can safely say that an indefinite number of fundamentals can be produced on a stringed instrument.

In addition to producing fundamentals, the string musician can touch the string lightly, without depressing it at all, and if the point where he touches it happens to be $\frac{1}{2}$, $\frac{1}{3}$, $\frac{1}{4}$, $\frac{1}{5}$ and so on of the length of the string, new notes will sound. Such notes are called harmonics.

In order to play harmonics successfully the player should bow *close to the bridge with sufficient pressure to produce a good tone. The amount of pressure is the same as for an open-string note.* He should set the finger precisely on the fractional division of the string. He should eliminate all pressure from the finger: the lighter it touches and the less space it covers, the clearer the harmonic.

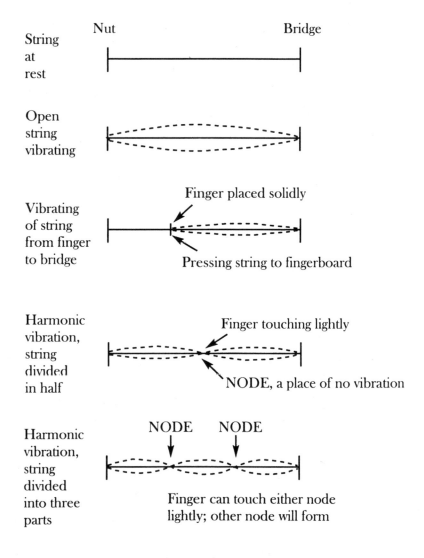

Figure 8-2. String vibration patterns.

Now let us look at the string as it forms itself into harmonic vibration. Figure 8-2 shows on the top line a string at rest. On the second line, the open string (full length of the string) is vibrating. The third line shows the finger pressing the string down to the fingerboard so that only the section between finger and bridge is vibrating--the string is sounding a fundamental. On the fourth line we see the first of the harmonic vibrations. The finger is touching the string lightly at its mid-point. Since the string is not depressed (not "stopped") the whole length of the string vibrates, but it vibrates in two parts due to the fact that the finger is touching it lightly in the middle thereby interfering with its vibration at that point. This place where the finger touches is called a node and it signifies that the string is standing still at that point.

Now look at the fifth line in the diagram. Notice that there are two nodes. The string is vibrating in three parts because the finger is touching lightly exactly one-third of the string's length. It does not make any difference which third is touched-the other node will form automatically and the pitch will be the same because we now have three little strings of the same length vibrating and therefore making, all three, the same pitch. Natural harmonics use the entire length of the string.

If the bow should happen to play right on a node, that harmonic could not form because the bow would not permit the string to stand still at that point. This is the reason why amateur bass players sometimes lose a harmonic after they have started it sounding--they let the bow slide away from the bridge and it gets on one of the nodes. Consequently, the harmonic disappears and nothing sounds.

This is not the place to go into the vast science of component harmonics (those that *color* the fundamental tones). We can only state that in bowing on nodes we eliminate such component harmonics from the tone color. This means that the artist string player has a control over his tone color that is unique among musical instruments. It is possible to make the violin assume the tone color of a flute or a clarinet--the former is a legitimate effect, but the latter is not practical since it means bowing the string at half its length, from finger to bridge.

The harmonics that are formed by dividing the string into fractions of its length are called the natural harmonics. These are spelled out for violin in the Table of Harmonics, Music Example 8-1. The series on any vibrating string is as follows: half the length of the string, octave; one-third the length of the string, fifth above the octave; one-fourth the length of the string, two octaves; one-fifth the string's length, the third (major) above the second octave.

In addition to the natural harmonics any fundamental can be turned into a harmonic sounding two octaves higher or an octave and a fifth higher by depressing the string with first finger on the fundamental (violin-viola) and then touching the same string lightly with the fourth finger or with fourth extended. The fourth finger divides the string into four parts, sounding two octaves high-

TABLE OF HARMONICS

PART ONE: NATURAL HARMONICS
Section 1
NOTATION I: Last Node Before Bridge

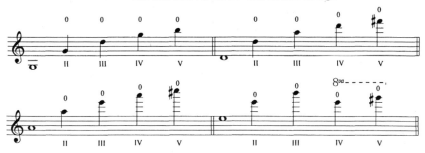

Section 2
NOTATION II: The Other Nodes

PART TWO: ARTIFICIAL HARMONICS

These may be formed on any pitch. Place first finger solidly on the desired pitch and touch the same string lightly with the fourth, or third finger as follows:

TYPE I: Easiest to perform. First finger solidly; fourth finger at the interval of a perfect fourth (its normal relationship to first finger). Sounds the first finger note two octaves above its written pitch.

TYPE II: Fourth finger stretched to reach a perfect fifth. Sounds an octave plus a fifth above the first finger note.

Music Example 8-1.

TYPE III: Third finger placed at a major third above first finger (two whole steps away). Sounds two octaves plus a major third above first finger note.

er than the fundamental; extended, into three parts sounding an octave and a fifth higher.

On cello the thumb with extended third finger is used for many of that instrument's artificial harmonics, the thumb making the fundamental, the finger producing the harmonic. On the bass the series of harmonics is myriad, but the player must remember to bow close to the bridge.

The notation for artificial harmonics is shown on the last three lines of the Table of Harmonics. The solid note states the fundamental, the diamond-shaped note, the harmonic finger. See also Appendix 9.

CLOSING REMARKS

When one arrives finally at the last page of a book such as this, one realizes that much that might have been said has been excluded. One can only hope that the material that has weathered the long period of refining is the essential material.

An attempt has been made throughout to relate cause and effect and to substantiate statements either through a process of logical reasoning or through the results of many years of experimentation with almost every known method of string teaching--and at all age levels from four to sixty. Literally thousands of beginners have made their contribution to string proficiency during those years. A life-time of practical study on all of the stringed instruments has yielded its harvest. With the violin ever in the ascendency, professional experience both in playing and teaching has added its values to the pedagogy.

In concluding this book, let us once more confirm our thesis that precise knowledge of what to do and how to do it is the basis of all fine teaching; that precise knowledge of what to do and how to do it is the basis of all intelligent learning; that dedication and loyalty to a musical purpose require hours of devotion in the form of practice to acquire the necessary skills; that knowledge alone will never play the notes nor make the music sound.

As a universal language music builds a deeply human understanding between one person and another, be it man to man or teacher to student, but to *speak* the language of Music — well, one has to do that for himself.

APPENDICES

BASIC PRINCIPLE FOR FINGERING THE STRINGED INSTRUMENTS

Whenever any one finger is resting on the string, the next whole tone higher in pitch will be located at one-twelfth of the remaining distance from that finger to the bridge. This means that as the hand shifts into the positions above first position, the fingers will fall progressively closer together.

FINGERING CHART–VIOLIN AND VIOLA
(First Position)

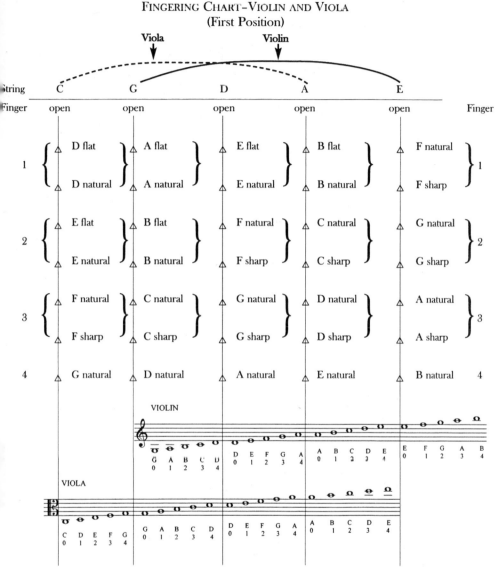

Note: In violin and viola, the finger changes when the letter-name of the note changes. When fingering a half-step, the fingers rest on the string so that they touch each other. In fingering a whole step, the fingers are approximately an inch apart on the string. A finger may play its own flat, natural, or sharp. To sharp a note, the finger extends toward the bridge approximately an inch. To flat a note, the finger reaches back toward the scroll approximately an inch. It will then rest against the finger behind it when that finger is on its natural. A finger sharping its note will rest on the same place, enharmonically, on the string which the next higher finger would occupy in flatting its note.

FINGERING CHART–CELLO (A)
(First Position–Normal)

String	C	G	D	A	
Finger	open	open	open	open	Finger
(Extension)					(Extension)
1 –	D flat	A flat	E flat	B flat	– 1
1 –	D natural	A natural	E natural	B natural	– 1
2 –	E flat	B flat	F natural	C natural	– 2
3 –	E natural	B natural	F sharp	C sharp	– 3
4 –	F natural	C natural	G natural	D natural	– 4

CELLO

Naturals	C D E F	G A B C	D E F G	A B C D
	0 1 2 3 4	0 1 2 3 4	0 1 2 3 4	0 1 2 3 4

Note: Notice that second and third fingers play the chromatic half step for the note which lies a third above the open string. Second finger plays the minor third, third finger the major third. First finger may extend backwards and upwards on the fingerboard to reach its flat (or, enharmonically, the open string sharp). From one finger to the next, consecutively, the fingers rest with approximately an inch of vacant space between them on the string. For the "extended" position of the hand, making it possible for the fourth finger to reach its sharp, see the next chart.

In normal non-extended position of the hand, consecutive fingers play half-steps.

FINGERING CHART–CELLO (B)
(First Position–Extended)

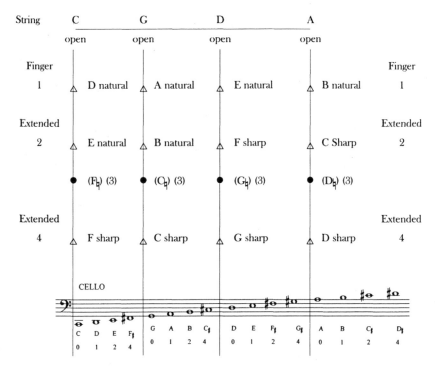

Note: In this extended position of the hand, the first finger to fourth finger covers a major third instead of a minor third as in the regular position. In this case, the second and fourth fingers each make an extension of a half tone more than their placing in the normal position. If the second finger fails to make the extension, the fourth finger will not play properly in tune with the normal hand. Notice, too, that in this position of extension, the fingers are resting on the string in the same *relative* position that they would occupy if the first finger were placed on the flat shown in the preceding chart for cello. In other words, the stretch between fingers is approximately the same regardless of whether the extension is backwards or forwards.

FINGERING CHART–STRING BASS (A)
(Half Position)

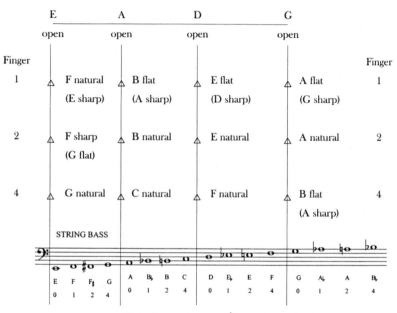

(Actually sound an octave lower than written)

Note: In fingering the string bass, the first, second, and fourth fingers only are used until the seventh position (thumb position). Each finger, consecutively, plays the next half step. It is of primary importance that the student make an early distinction between half position and first position. When the first finger is resting on the note one-half tone higher than the open string, the hand is then in the half position. When the first finger rests on the note which is a whole tone higher than the open string, the hand is then in the first position. The thumb should remain in back of the second finger at all times. This means that the thumb will move down the neck of the instrument approximately two inches as the hand shifts from half to first position. The fingers one-four span one whole tone on any one string in any one position on the bass. For the first position fingering, see the next chart.

When the octave harmonic is reached on any string, the third finger comes into use.

It often plays this harmonic. When the thumb is placed on the octave harmonic, the THUMB POSITION is then functioning. Fingering then becomes thumb, one, two, three. Fourth is not used. From seventh position up, fingering is similar to the violin fingering.

FINGERING CHART–STRING BASS (B)
(First Position)

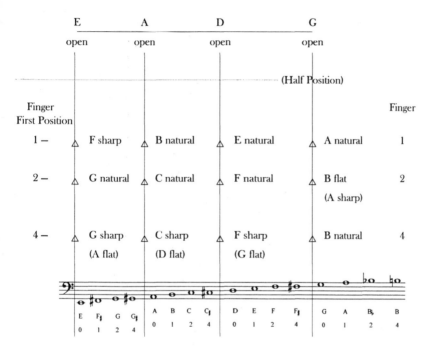

	E	A	D	G	
	open	open	open	open	
			(Half Position)		
Finger First Position					Finger
1 —	F sharp	B natural	E natural	A natural	1
2 —	G natural	C natural	F natural	B flat (A sharp)	2
4 —	G sharp (A flat)	C sharp (D flat)	F sharp (G flat)	B natural	4

Note: In general, the first position is used for keys in sharps and the half position is used when the signature is in flats. Also, in general, when three or more sharps or three or more flats appear in the signature, it will be necessary for the left hand to shift frequently and fluently between the two positions. Be sure the thumb makes the shift by dropping or rising the necessary two inches as required. When the bass student begins in a homogeneous class, it is best to learn the half position thoroughly first. But in the heterogeneous class there is only one solution, which is to start the basses in the first position for the sake of conformity to the other instruments.

Seating Plan for Elementary School Orchestra

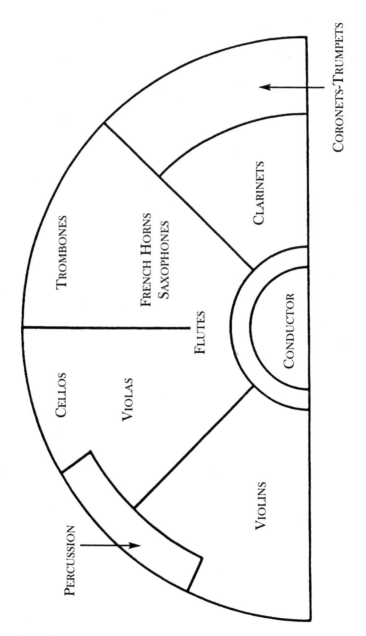

Elizabeth A.H. Green, *The Modern Conductor*, 4/E, © 1987, pp. 132, 232.
Reprinted by permission of Prentice-Hall, Inc., Englewood Cliffs, New Jersey.

PHYSICAL AND PSYCHOLOGICAL ASPECTS OF MUSICAL TRAINING

a) **Elementary level:** These factors must be trained one at a time. but with an over-all picture in the teacher's mind so that all factors receive the necessary development.

(b) **Advanced level:** The problem is to devise a method where all factors work efficiently, effectively, and simultaneously during practice and performance.

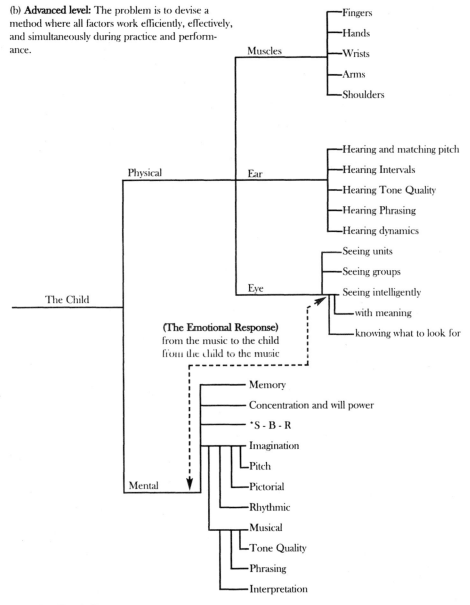

The Child

Physical

Muscles
- Fingers
- Hands
- Wrists
- Arms
- Shoulders

Ear
- Hearing and matching pitch
- Hearing Intervals
- Hearing Tone Quality
- Hearing Phrasing
- Hearing dynamics

Eye
- Seeing units
- Seeing groups
- Seeing intelligently
- with meaning
- knowing what to look for

(The Emotional Response)
from the music to the child
from the child to the music

Mental
- Memory
- Concentration and will power
- *S - B - R
- Imagination
  - Pitch
  - Pictorial
  - Rhythmic
- Musical
  - Tone Quality
  - Phrasing
- Interpretation

*Stimulus - Bond - Response

POSITIONS CHART–VIOLIN

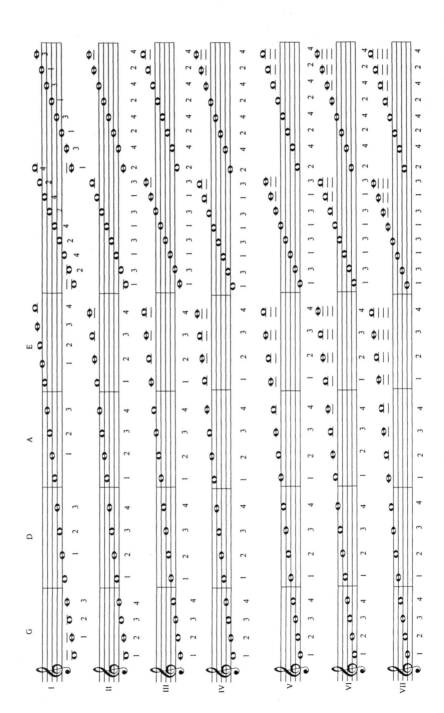

OUTLINE OF HARMONICS: VIOLIN, VIOLA, CELLO, AND STRING BASS

The *natural harmonics* divide the entire length of the string, from nut to bridge, into aliquot parts. When the composer desires the player to finger the last node before the bridge, he writes the customary note plus a zero indication above it. When a node other than this may be fingered, the diamond-shaped note is used.

In the following outline, *all notes are to be played on the A string of the several instruments.*

Using the **Open String** as the **Root:**

As a harmonic: $\frac{1}{2}$ the length of the string <u>sounds</u> the octave of the root. Tune the finger on the octave of the open string; then lighten the finger-pressure to sound the harmonic.

As a harmonic: $\frac{1}{3}$ the length of the string <u>sounds</u> the fifth above the octave. Tune the finger on the note a perfect fifth above the open string; then lighten the pressure to sound the harmonic.

As a harmonic: $\frac{1}{4}$ the length of the string <u>sounds</u> the second octave above the open string. Tune the finger on the note a perfect fourth above the open string; then lighten the pressure to sound the harmonic.

As a harmonic: $\frac{1}{5}$ the length of the string <u>sounds</u> the major third above the second octave of the open string: tune the finger on the note a major third (or major sixth) above the open string; then lighten the pressure to sound the harmonic.

Note: In all of the above notations, remember that the string bass sounds an octave lower than notated throughout.

Setting the fingers on corresponding intervals on the other strings will produce corresponding harmonic sounds, related to the open string as a root. The resulting <u>sounds</u> for the fractional divisions on each string are as follows:

	½	⅓	¼	⅕
E string:	E	B	E	G-sharp
A string:	A	E	A	C-sharp
D string:	D	A	D	F-sharp
G string:	G	D	G	B-natural
C string:	C	G	C	E-natural

The Artificial Harmonics:

Any note may be turned into an artificial harmonic as follows: Place one finger solidly on the notated black note and touch the same string lightly with another finger on the diamond-shaped note.

Breaks string into:

	four parts	three parts	five parts
Sounds:	2 octaves above black note	twelfth above black note (i.e., octave above diamond-shaped note)	2 octave above diamond-shaped note

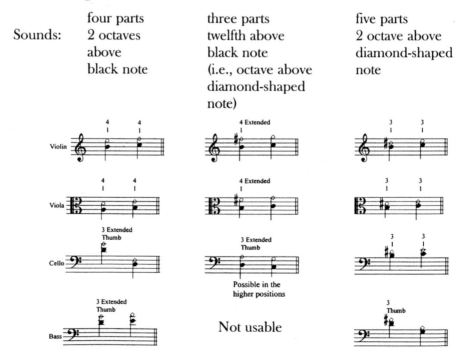

Note: Artificial harmonics are impractical on the bass below the third position because of the enormous span needed between the two notes, but they may be played in the higher-numbered positions.

In the foregoing outline it will be seen that harmonics up to the division of the string into five parts are useful. Divisions into six parts (sounding the fifth in the third octave above the root), seven parts (sounding an out-of-tune seventh in the third octave), and eight parts (sounding the fourth octave of the root), are all playable, especially on the larger instruments. However, the division into six parts requires that the finger making the harmonic sound be placed on a quarter-tone interval (between the major and minor third)–and our system of musical notation has not solved this problem as yet. The string bass finds such a division useful as an artificial harmonic performed with the thumb and *second* finger in the higher-numbered positions.

INDEX